I0447452

July 2011

BURMA

UN and U.S. Agencies Assisted Cyclone Victims in Difficult Environment, but Improved U.S. Monitoring Needed

Highlights of GAO-11-700, a report to congressional committees

Why GAO Did This Study

Cyclone Nargis hit Burma's impoverished Irrawaddy Delta on May 2, 2008, leaving nearly 140,000 people dead or missing and severely affecting about 2.4 million others, according to the UN. The Burmese military government initially blocked most access to the affected region; however, amid international pressure, it slowly began allowing international aid workers entry into the region. Since 1997, the United States has imposed sanctions to prohibit, among other things, the exportation of financial services to Burma and transactions with Burmese officials. In response to a congressional mandate, GAO (1) described the assistance UN and U.S. agencies have provided in response to Cyclone Nargis, (2) assessed USAID actions to help ensure funds are used as intended and do not benefit sanctioned entities, and (3) described the challenges responders experienced and the lessons learned. GAO reviewed financial and program documents; interviewed U.S., UN, and nongovernmental organization (NGO) officials; and traveled to Thailand and Burma.

What GAO Recommends

GAO recommends that the Administrator of USAID (1) take four actions to improve the management of grants related to Burma, including enhancing financial monitoring and reinforcing the requirement to document site visits, and (2) review the questionable costs for international travel GAO identified. USAID concurred with GAO's recommendations.

View GAO-11-700 or key components. For more information, contact Thomas Melito at (202) 512-9601 or melitot@gao.gov.

What GAO Found

UN and U.S. agencies provided about $335 million for emergency response and recovery activities after Cyclone Nargis. Of that total, 11 UN agencies obligated roughly $288 million for assistance in various sectors, including food, health, water and sanitation, and agriculture. The U.S. government provided about $38 million of the UN's total as part of its roughly $85 million in obligations for emergency response and longer-term recovery activities. Of the $85 million U.S. response, the U.S. Agency for International Development (USAID), which led U.S. efforts, obligated about $72 million. The Department of Defense obligated about $13 million to procure and deliver emergency relief supplies. (See our video clip showing conditions shortly after Cyclone Nargis.)

USAID took actions to help ensure U.S. funds were used as intended and did not benefit sanctioned entities, but had some monitoring weaknesses. USAID took actions prior to the delivery of assistance, including selecting partners experienced in working with USAID and in Burma and providing extra guidance to help ensure funds were not misused. To monitor assistance, USAID has conducted some site visits. However, USAID's monitoring contains little financial oversight and we found that two grantees charged USAID for unapproved international travel. Also, in some cases site visits were not sufficiently documented. USAID relies on external audits of grantees, but relevant USAID staff were not aware of audit findings related to one grantee's cash payments to villagers in Burma. The grantee subsequently addressed the audit findings. Lastly, U.S. and UN agencies said they examined reports of misuse of assistance in their programs and found no evidence that assistance had been misused.

GAO's review of 16 after-action reports from donors, NGOs, and UN agencies, showed that those responding to Cyclone Nargis experienced similar challenges and developed lessons learned in four main areas: access, coordination, implementation, and limited in-country disaster response capacity. Responders found it difficult to reach affected areas because the Burmese government limited their travel and the infrastructure was poor. Responders also had difficulty coordinating between headquarters and field offices for several reasons, including limited telecommunication services. A U.S. report highlighted coordination challenges amongst U.S. agencies, stating that agencies' conflicting agendas resulted in difficulties related to the appropriateness, timing, procurement, and distribution of aid. Implementation challenges include supplies that were incompatible with local conditions, such as medicines with instructions printed in non-Burmese languages and difficulties monitoring aid. Capacity challenges included a lack of experienced disaster specialists in Burma, which resulted in nonqualified individuals being placed in positions out of necessity. To address some of these challenges, reports suggested that organizations increase support staff and use the same reporting systems. Other reports prioritized involving local communities in decision making and improving emergency preparedness and local response capacity.

_____ United States Government Accountability Office

Contents

Abbreviations

AO	Agreement Officer
AOTR	Agreement Officer's Technical Representative
ASEAN	Association of Southeast Asian Nations
DOD	U.S. Department of Defense
FAO	Food and Agriculture Organization of the United Nations
NGO	Nongovernmental organization
OFAC	Office of Foreign Asset Controls, U.S Treasury Department
OFDA	Office of Foreign Disaster Assistance, USAID
RDMA	Regional Development Mission for Asia, USAID
State	U.S. Department of State
TCG	Tripartite Core Group
Treasury	Department of the Treasury
UN	United Nations
UN OCHA	UN Office for the Coordination of Humanitarian Affairs
UNDP	United Nations Development Program
UNICEF	United Nations Children's Fund
USAID	U.S. Agency for International Development
WFP	World Food Program

View GAO Components

Video of Cyclone Nargis's destruction in the delta region

United States Government Accountability Office
Washington, DC 20548

July 26, 2011

The Honorable Patrick Leahy
Chairman
The Honorable Lindsey Graham
Ranking Member
Subcommittee on State, Foreign Operations,
    and Related Programs
Committee on Appropriations
United States Senate

The Honorable Kay Granger
Chairwoman
The Honorable Nita Lowey
Ranking Member
Subcommittee on State, Foreign Operations,
    and Related Programs
Committee on Appropriations
House of Representatives

Cyclone Nargis hit Burma's impoverished Irrawaddy Delta on May 2, 2008, leaving nearly 140,000 people dead or missing and severely affecting about 2.4 million others, according to the United Nations (UN) Office for the Coordination of Humanitarian Affairs (UN OCHA).[1] In response, UN OCHA reports that the international community mobilized more than $600 million in aid as of May 2011, including $334.8 million from U.S. and UN agencies.[2] The Burmese military government initially blocked most international access to the affected region; however, amidst international pressure, it slowly began allowing aid to be delivered throughout May 2008 and finally allowed international aid workers into the cyclone-affected delta by late May 2008. The United States has provided funds for Cyclone Nargis emergency response and recovery activities largely through UN agencies and international nongovernmental

---

[1]Burma is also known as Myanmar.

[2]As reported through UN OCHA's Financial Tracking System as of May 2011. The other approximately $278 million of the more than $600 million total includes funding from international donors, such as the United Kingdom, Australia, Japan, the European Commission, and private donors.

GAO-11-700 Burma

organizations (NGO). The U.S. Agency for International Development (USAID) has funded most of the U.S. response and recovery activities. The Department of Defense (DOD) provided emergency supplies, direct air transport, and logistics support. The U.S. Department of State (State) played a role in coordinating and monitoring the U.S. government response.

In 1997, the United States prohibited new investment in Burma and has since imposed broad sanctions to prohibit the exportation of financial services to Burma,[3] certain imports from Burma, and transactions with senior Burmese officials and others,[4] and has provided limited assistance to Burma. The sanctions arise from actions and policies by the Burmese military government that repress the democratic opposition in Burma. The U.S. Department of the Treasury (Treasury) implements many elements of the sanctions program, including the prohibitions on exports of financial services to Burma and the targeted financial prohibitions. Congressional committees mandated that we assess the assistance that the United States provided in response to the cyclone.[5] To address the mandate, in this report we (1) describe the assistance UN and U.S. agencies have provided in response to Cyclone Nargis, (2) assess USAID actions to help ensure funds are used as intended and do not benefit sanctioned entities,

---

[3]The Department of the Treasury's Office of Foreign Assets Control (OFAC) issued a general license for organizations to export financial services to Burma that are not otherwise authorized, in order to support not-for-profit humanitarian or religious activities in Burma (OFAC Amended General License No. 14-B). The license prohibits exports of financial services, either directly or indirectly, to the Government of Burma. In addition, OFAC has granted USAID and State a specific license which allows U.S. government grantees in Burma to transfer funds that are in direct support of activities defined and authorized by their U.S. government grants and contracts. This license would authorize assistance for sanctioned entities, including the Government of Burma, if they were contained within the scope of a grantee's agreement with the U.S. government. However, USAID reported that their agreements generally do not authorize assistance for the Government of Burma or sanctioned entities.

[4]The sanctions were developed through a series of federal laws and executive orders, many of which block property and interests in property of certain entities and individuals in Burma. In addition to senior Burmese government officials designated by OFAC, sanctions also apply to any Burmese persons who provide substantial economic and political support for the Burmese government who are on OFAC's list of Specially Designated Nationals and Blocked Persons (Pub. L. No. 110-286, § 5(d) (2008); Pres. Det. 2009-11 (Jan. 15, 2009)).

[5]H.R. Rep. 111-151, at 128 (2009).

and (3) describe the challenges responders experienced and the lessons learned.

To address these objectives, we reviewed financial and program documents from USAID, DOD, State, Treasury, UN agencies, and NGOs. We also interviewed U.S., UN, and NGO officials in Washington, D.C.; Bangkok, Thailand; and Rangoon, Burma; and conducted site visits to select USAID-funded recovery projects in Burma. To address the first objective, we reviewed relevant documents, including grants, cooperative agreements, and progress reports. We interviewed U.S. and UN officials and conducted site visits. To address the second objective, we reviewed program and financial files for funds USAID awarded in response to Cyclone Nargis and spoke with USAID officials about their monitoring of programs. We also conducted a limited internal controls review of three NGOs, which collectively account for 66 percent of funding that USAID awarded to international NGOs to respond to Cyclone Nargis. We also met with officials from these three NGOs and with USAID officials responsible for financial oversight of the NGOs' programs. To address the third objective, we reviewed 16 relevant after-action and assessment reports prepared by the U.S. government, UN agencies, and NGOs to identify challenges experienced during the Cyclone Nargis response, as well as lessons learned. We also interviewed U.S., UN, and NGO officials.

We conducted this performance audit from July 2010 through July 2011 in accordance with generally accepted government auditing standards. Those standards require that we plan and perform the audit to obtain sufficient, appropriate evidence to provide a reasonable basis for our findings and conclusions based on our audit objectives. We believe that the evidence obtained provides a reasonable basis for our findings and conclusions based on our audit objectives. See appendix I for a more detailed discussion of our scope and methodology.

In this report, we recommend that the Administrator of USAID direct the appropriate mission and offices to improve management of grants related to Burma by taking actions, such as (1) enhancing financial monitoring of agreements by including periodic reviews of grantee internal controls, transactions, and disbursement records; (2) providing grantees with specific guidance on the approval process for international travel requests, and ensuring that USAID staff monitor grantees' expenditures for compliance with related laws, regulations, and grant agreements, including international travel; (3) reinforcing the requirement for staff to formally document site visits to grantees; and (4) ensuring all relevant offices are made aware of audit findings in a timely manner. We also recommend that the Administrator of USAID direct the appropriate mission and offices to follow-up on the questionable costs associated with international travel that we identified in this report and take action as appropriate on any identified unallowable costs. USAID concurred with all recommendations.

Background

Cyclone Nargis Severely Affected More than 3 Million Burmese

Cyclone Nargis left nearly 140,000 people dead or missing, up to 800,000 displaced, and roughly 2.4 million severely affected.[6] The strong tropical cyclone struck Burma's impoverished Irrawaddy Delta on May 2, 2008, with a storm surge of 12 feet and continued east-northeast through the Rangoon division (see fig. 1).

---

[6]As reported in UN OCHA's *Myanmar Revised Appeal, Cyclone Nargis Response Plan* (July 2008).

Figure 1: Map of Cyclone Nargis Path through Burma

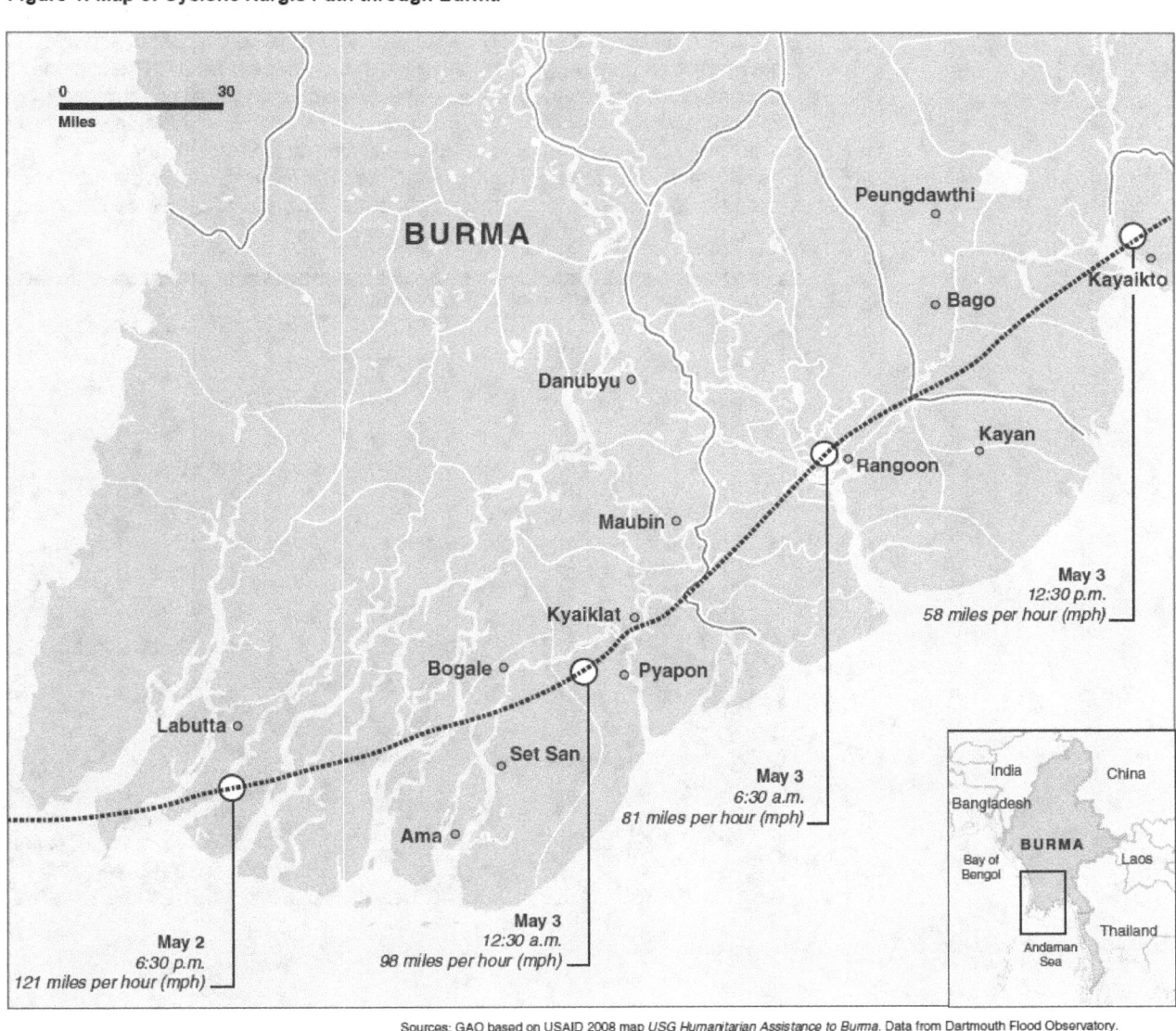

Sources: GAO based on USAID 2008 map *USG Humanitarian Assistance to Burma*. Data from Dartmouth Flood Observatory.

Strong winds and heavy rainfall led to the flooding of inland areas and agricultural lands, the destruction of 450,000 homes, and the devastation of food stocks, livelihoods, and infrastructure, according to the Tripartite Core

Group joint assessment.[7] For examples of Cyclone Nargis's destruction in the delta region, see figure 2 and our video. The assessment stated that the cyclone destroyed or severely damaged more than 50 percent of schools and nearly 75 percent of health facilities in the affected areas. The cyclone also impaired access to clean water because the salt water contaminated communal water collection systems and destroyed household rainwater collection containers. Prior to the cyclone, Burma had significant humanitarian needs resulting from decades of chronic underinvestment in essential services by the Burmese government, ongoing ethnic conflict, and government policies that stifle economic growth.

Figure 2: Cyclone Destruction in the Delta Region

Source: DOD.

---

[7]Tripartite Core Group, *Post-Nargis Joint Assessment* (July 2008).

Burmese Government Restricted Access to Cyclone-Affected Areas but Some Aid Was Delivered

In the week following the cyclone, the Government of Burma said it was accepting international aid but was not ready to accept international aid workers, insisting that the disaster could be handled internally and therefore they did not need experts. Due to the inability to enter Burma, many foreign donors, including the U.S. government, began assembling staff in Bangkok, Thailand, to be ready for quick deployment if granted access. The U.S. and other donors also had military ships anchored off the coast of Burma, ready to supply humanitarian assistance if allowed by the Burmese government.

The Government of Burma restricted the movement of the few international aid workers who were in Burma when the cyclone hit as well as those it eventually allowed to enter the country. The Burmese Government has had a longstanding policy requiring approval for any international staff to travel outside of Rangoon.[8] Within the first two weeks after the cyclone struck, the government set up military checkpoints outside of Rangoon, blocking access to the cyclone-affected areas for anyone without the proper travel approvals.

Despite the inability of international aid workers to get into Burma and government restrictions on the movement of international aid workers within Burma, some aid was delivered. International agencies already in Burma launched operations within a few days, working through their local staff or in partnership with local organizations. The Burmese government provided some assistance to cyclone-affected areas. One U.S. official reported that the Burmese military set up a logistics center in Rangoon and delivered some relief supplies. One report also suggested that the Burmese army and navy rescued some people stranded in remote areas; set up camps for displaced people; and restored some electricity, communication, and transportation links.[9]

Burmese citizens and local organizations also assisted cyclone victims. According to the same report, within hours of the cyclone, the first local

---

[8]Rangoon is the former capital of Burma, and its largest city. In 2005, Burma's ruling regime unexpectedly relocated the capital city from Rangoon to Nay Pyi Taw, further isolating the government from the public and international community. Nay Pyi Taw is sparsely populated, and rapid development of the new capital continues. Foreign diplomatic missions remain in Rangoon, according to State.

[9]International Crisis Group, *Burma/Myanmar After Nargis: Time to Normalize Aid Relations*, Asia Report N°161 (Oct. 20, 2008).

response efforts were underway, led by monks, doctors, students, artists, intellectuals, travel agents, and small business owners. Several hundred new and existing groups, including a contingent of Burmese citizens returning from abroad, provided relief. While most of the larger international agencies initially focused on the main population centers, many of these small, informal groups assisted the most isolated areas. Several officials cited the local response as one of the main reasons there was not a further loss of life in the weeks immediately following the cyclone; however, they reported that the local response was exhausting its supplies by the end of May 2008.

Tripartite Core Group Formed to Facilitate Response

Under pressure by the international community and UN entities to allow international aid workers access to affected populations, the Burmese government pledged on May 23, 2008, during a visit by the UN Secretary General, that it would begin granting international aid workers access to Burma and the cyclone-affected regions. The Association of South East Asian Nations (ASEAN),[10] of which Burma is a member, played a leading role in getting international disaster response workers into Burma. ASEAN took the lead in coordinating assistance offered by the international community, with full support from the UN, and in late May 2008 formed the Tripartite Core Group (TCG). The TCG's mission was to facilitate trust, confidence, and cooperation between the Government of Burma and the international community on matters concerning Cyclone Nargis humanitarian relief and recovery work. The TCG consisted of three members from the Burmese government, three from ASEAN, and three from the UN. The TCG started its work on May 31, 2008, and met once a week until its mandate ended in July 2010. The TCG facilitated the issuance of visas and permits to travel, as well as visa extensions for UN and foreign aid workers. The TCG also led the post-Nargis Joint Assessment, conducted in June 2008, and helped facilitate the entry and deployment of 10 commercial helicopters used in conducting assessments and delivering relief supplies.

---

[10]ASEAN's goals include accelerating economic growth, social progress, and cultural development in the region through joint endeavors in the spirit of equality and partnership. Indonesia, Malaysia, Philippines, Singapore, and Thailand established ASEAN in 1967. Burma, Brunei Darussalam, Cambodia, Lao PDR, and Vietnam subsequently joined.

U.S. Government Has Imposed Sanctions on Burma Since 1997

Since 1997 the U.S. government has imposed sanctions on Burma mainly due to the ruling Burmese military regime's actions and policies.[11] The State Law and Order Restoration Council (later known as the State Peace and Development Council) that took power in 1988 has routinely restricted freedom of speech, religion, and movement and committed other serious human rights violations against the Burmese people. It has condoned the use of forced labor and taken military action against ethnic minorities living within the country. Burma's ruling regime has also periodically blocked or impeded activities undertaken by UN and international NGOs in Burma, as we previously reported.[12] In 1990, national parliamentary elections resulted in an overwhelming victory for the National League for Democracy party, led by Aung San Suu Kyi. However, the ruling State Law and Order Restoration Council refused to yield power and maintained its policies of autocratic rule.

Parliamentary elections held in November 2010—described by a U.S. government source as "flawed"—saw the ruling regime's party garner more than 75 percent of the seats. Parliament convened in January 2011 and selected the former Prime Minister as President. The government source reported that the vast majority of national-level appointees named by the new President are former or current military officers.

The current U.S. sanctions against Burma limit, among other things, the export of financial services by U.S. persons or from the United States to Burma and new U.S. investment in Burma. The Treasury's Office of Foreign Assets Control (OFAC) manages the U.S. sanctions program by issuing licenses, monitoring compliance, and bringing enforcement actions against violators of the sanctions. The sanctions have developed through laws, such as the Burmese Freedom and Democracy Act of 2003 and the Tom Lantos Block Burmese JADE (Junta's Anti-Democratic Efforts) Act of 2008, as well as through presidential executive orders. U.S. law also requires that the United States withhold a share of its voluntary contributions to most UN organizations proportionate to their funding for

---

[11]Australia, Canada, and the European Union have joined the United States in imposing sanctions against Burma's regime.

[12]GAO, *International Organizations: Assistance Constrained in Burma*, GAO-07-457 (Washington, D.C.: Apr. 6, 2007).

programs in Burma.[13] Generally, aid donated to Burma on behalf of the United States is not intended to benefit sanctioned entities, such as senior Burmese government officials or persons associated with the military regime that have been designated as such by OFAC. Further, State identifies Burma as a "major illicit drug producing country" that has failed to adhere to its obligations under international counter-narcotics agreements and is, therefore, banned from receiving some U.S. aid under the Foreign Assistance Act of 1961.[14]

To operate legally in Burma, USAID used funds provided with notwithstanding authority[15] and obtained OFAC licenses. Notwithstanding authority allowed USAID to provide humanitarian assistance to Burma despite other provisions of law limiting agencies' ability to operate in Burma. This authority automatically applied to USAID's Office of Foreign Disaster Assistance (USAID/OFDA) programs because the law allows for international disaster assistance, including relief and rehabilitation, to be provided notwithstanding any other provision of law. Other appropriations were also provided with notwithstanding authority to fund humanitarian assistance in Burma for individuals and communities impacted by the cyclone.[16] OFAC licenses have allowed USAID and its grantees and contractors to operate in Burma, in order to conduct financial transactions and other activities otherwise prohibited by the U.S. sanctions.

---

[13]Members fund UN agencies through voluntary contributions, assessed contributions, or both. Voluntary contributions are decided on by each country, and they finance special UN programs and offices, such as the UN Development Program and the UN Children's Fund. The U.S. federal law that requires withholding the U.S. proportionate share for programs in Burma does not apply to the UN Children's Fund. In contrast, member countries are required to pay their assessed contributions for UN organizations.

[14]22 U.S.C. § 2291j, 22 U.S.C. § 2291j-1; Presidential Determination No. 2009-30, 74 Fed. Reg. 48369 (Sept. 15, 2009).

[15]22 U.S.C. § 2292(b).

[16]Supplemental Appropriations Act, 2009, Pub. L. No. 111-32, 123 Stat. 1859, 1892 (June 24, 2009).

UN and U.S. Agencies Obligated About $335 Million in Assistance to Burma after Cyclone Nargis

In response to the humanitarian crisis in Burma following Cyclone Nargis, UN and U.S. agencies obligated roughly $334.8 million in assistance, as of March 2011. Of this total, the UN obligated $288 million and the United States obligated $84.6 million—$37.8 million of which went to UN agencies, and is therefore included in the UN total as well. Of the remaining U.S. assistance, $33.9 million was provided through NGOs and $12.9 million was provided by DOD.

UN Agencies Obligated $288 Million for Emergency Response and Recovery Assistance

UN agencies played a critical role in implementing international assistance in response to Cyclone Nargis. Eleven UN agencies obligated $288 million since 2008, $37.8 million (13 percent) of which came from U.S. funding,[17] and provided emergency response and recovery assistance.[18] The UN, through the acting Humanitarian Coordinator and the country team, organized the emergency and early recovery phase of the Cyclone Nargis response and assigned UN agencies and NGOs lead responsibility for particular relief sectors, as shown in figure 3, an interactive graphic. (See app. II for mission descriptions of the UN agencies.)

---

[17]USAID provided funding to 7 of the 11 UN agencies. The four UN agencies that did not receive U.S. funding are the Food and Agriculture Organization; International Labor Organization; United Nations Educational, Scientific, and Cultural Organization; and the United Nations Population Fund.

[18]All UN agency funding obligations are as reported in UN OCHA's Financial Tracking Service. See http://fts.unocha.org/. The tracking service makes efforts to collect and report all humanitarian assistance. However, it guarantees only that suitable humanitarian funding information sent to it will be posted; the tracking service cannot guarantee that it will find and record information not sent to it. Given this limitation, it is possible that we may have underreported total UN obligations.

Figure 3: UN Assistance by Sector, 2008 through March 2011

Interactive instructions:

The online version of this matrix is interactive. Hover your mouse over each UN organization for a description of that organization.

To view these descriptions in the offline version, see appendix II.

	Obligations (millions of U.S. dollars)	Agriculture	Early recovery/ livelihoods	Education	Shelter	Emergency telecommunications	Food	Health	Logistics/emergency relief supplies	Nutrition	Protection	Water, sanitation, and hygiene
World Food Program (WFP)	$129.4					L	L		L			
United Nations Children's Fund (UNICEF)	$79.3		L	✓				✓		L	✓	L
United Nations Development Program (UNDP)	$33.9	✓	L					✓				✓
Food & Agriculture Organization of the United Nations (FAO)	$17.2	L										
United Nations High Commissioner for Refugees (UNHCR)	$9.7			✓							L	
World Health Organization (WHO)	$8.7							L				
Office for the Coordination of Humanitarian Affairs (UN OCHA)[a]	$4.5											
International Labor Organization (ILO)	$2.3		✓									
United Nations Population Fund (UNFPA)	$1.9							✓			✓	
United Nations Educational, Scientific and Cultural Organization (UNESCO)	$0.6			✓								
United Nations Human Settlements Program (UN-HABITAT)	$0.5				L							
Total funding	**$288.0**											

L Lead responsibility for the sector; also provided assistance

✓ Provided assistance

Source: GAO analysis of UN data.

Note: Certain sectors had more than one lead agency, and the lead positions sometimes changed over time. In addition, sectors, such as education and health, had NGOs as co-leads.

[a] UN OCHA provided a broad array of coordiantion assistance across the sectors.

Four UN agencies—the World Food Program (WFP), United Nations Children's Fund (UNICEF), United Nations Development Program (UNDP), and the Food and Agriculture Organization of the United Nations (FAO)—contributed approximately 90 percent of the $288 million. Nearly half of the total funding came through WFP, which distributed food and supplied common services, such as providing trucks and cargo vessels for transporting humanitarian assistance, to the UN and other responding agencies. These four UN agencies provided the following activities and services:

- *WFP.* As the UN's largest assistance provider for this humanitarian emergency and the lead agency responsible for the food, logistics, and telecommunications sectors, WFP obligated nearly $130 million for associated activities, as of March 2011. WFP distributed food in the Irrawaddy Delta and Rangoon Division, reaching nearly one million people and supplying more than 70,000 tons of food according to WFP reports. The food commodities included rice, beans, vegetable oil, salt, ready-to-eat meals, and high-energy biscuits. In urban areas of the Rangoon Division, where markets remained viable, WFP conducted a cash transfer program that provided cash assistance to purchase a week's worth of food to more than 49,000 beneficiaries. However, the Burmese government cancelled this program in June 2008. According to WFP officials, the Burmese government maintained that the cash transfer program had a negative impact on the economy because it used informal rather than formal exchange rates.[19] In August 2008, following the termination of the project, WFP began providing food rations for 131,400 Rangoon beneficiaries. In fall 2008, WFP and its partners began to shift their focus from relief food provision to early recovery efforts in order to establish opportunities for work and livelihood redevelopment—principally in the occupations of farming and fishing.

  In addition to food assistance, WFP helped supply and coordinate common services to the UN and other responding agencies. WFP established five logistics hubs across the delta to provide forward locations for temporary food storage prior to distribution, and bases for transportation to onward destinations by road, waterways, or air. Upon completion of air operations in August 2008, WFP reported that

---

[19]According to WFP, UN agencies, NGOs, and businesses in Burma generally used the common market exchange rate of around 1,100 Burmese kyat to one U.S. dollar—the exchange rate at the time of the crisis. Use of the official and highly over-valued exchange rate of 6 kyat to one U.S. dollar would have made all UN operations too costly, according to WFP.

it had transported 4,177 tons of food and relief supplies from the UN staging area in Bangkok. Helicopters delivered 1,088 tons of emergency food and nonfood items to 160 remote locations. Because the delta is a labyrinth of waterways, WFP contracted a fleet of barges, push tugs, and river boats, which various agencies used to transport an additional 10,405 tons of humanitarian supplies, as well as trucks for inland travel.

- *UNICEF.* UNICEF led three sectors—education; nutrition; and water, sanitation, and hygiene—and obligated more than $79 million for associated activities, as of March 2011. UNICEF reported that strong winds and heavy rainfall from Cyclone Nargis left more than 4,000 schools and more than 600 health facilities destroyed or badly damaged. As a result, their immediate priorities included preventing disease outbreaks, ensuring availability of safe drinking water, establishing temporary learning spaces for children, creating child-friendly spaces for traumatized children, and tracing and reintegrating the families of separated children. UNICEF said it constructed and maintained 300 emergency latrines, installed 558 large rainwater containers and 8 water treatment plants, administered more than 110,000 measles vaccinations to children in cyclone-affected areas and deployed health assistants to severely affected townships, provided school kits to 2,322 schools to facilitate resuming of the school year and renovated 965 schools and 702 staff houses, and supported 27,000 children through a range of care and protection activities in 272 locations in 13 affected townships.

- *UNDP.* As the lead agency for the early recovery sector, UNDP was the only UN agency with project offices located in the delta region prior to Cyclone Nargis. UNDP's eight project offices and associated staff helped distribute supplies, such as water, food, plastic sheets, cooking utensils, medicine, and clothing. UNDP obligated nearly $34 million, as of March 2011, and adapted its pre-cyclone Human Development Initiative projects to meet the early recovery needs of Cyclone Nargis survivors, focusing primarily on livelihood re-establishment, but also including grass-roots interventions in the areas of primary health care, the environment, HIV/AIDS, training and education, and food security. UNDP also adapted its micro-enterprise/micro-credit program to support enterprise creation and rehabilitation, including helping affected populations to rebuild their houses.

- *FAO.* To restore and strengthen food security by helping to restore livelihoods in agriculture and fisheries production in Burma's cyclone-affected provinces, FAO obligated about $17 million, as of March

2011. As the lead agency for the agriculture sector, FAO provided crop, vegetable, and fruit seedlings; fertilizers; technical assistance for crop and livestock production; improved fishing techniques; fish processing equipment; livestock and fisheries inputs; veterinary equipment; and animal vaccinations.

U.S. Government Responded to Cyclone Nargis with Nearly $85 Million in Assistance

In response to Cyclone Nargis, the U.S. government obligated $84.6 million since May 2008—$74.9 million for emergency response activities and $9.7 million for longer-term recovery assistance. Of the total funds obligated, USAID obligated $71.7 million, of which $37.8 million went to UN programs, and DOD obligated $12.9 million. U.S. assistance covered multiple sectors throughout the delta region; however, certain townships received a more extensive range of assistance.[20] (See app. III for a map that shows the location and type of emergency assistance that U.S. agencies provided in response to Cyclone Nargis.)

U.S. Emergency Response Prioritized Relief Supplies

As the lead agency for the U.S. government's response to Cyclone Nargis, USAID/OFDA established a disaster assistance response team in the region within days after the cyclone struck. USAID/OFDA also immediately provided $250,000 to UN agencies for emergency assistance. Due to the delay in the Burmese government's issuance of visas, USAID deployed the disaster response team to Bangkok, and a logistics team established operations in Utapao, Thailand.[21]

The U.S. government's emergency response consisted of $33.9 million in assistance from USAID/OFDA, $28.1 million in food aid assistance from USAID's Office of Food for Peace, and $12.9 million in assistance from DOD, as shown in figure 4.

---

[20]The townships of Bogale, Labutta, Mawlamyinegyun, and Ngapudaw received the most extensive range of assistance, covering at least four of the seven relief sectors the U.S. funded.

[21]Although disaster response team members requested visas within days after the cyclone struck, the Burmese regime granted some but not all visas in late May 2008.

Figure 4: U.S. Emergency Response Obligations by Sector, Fiscal Years 2008 and 2009

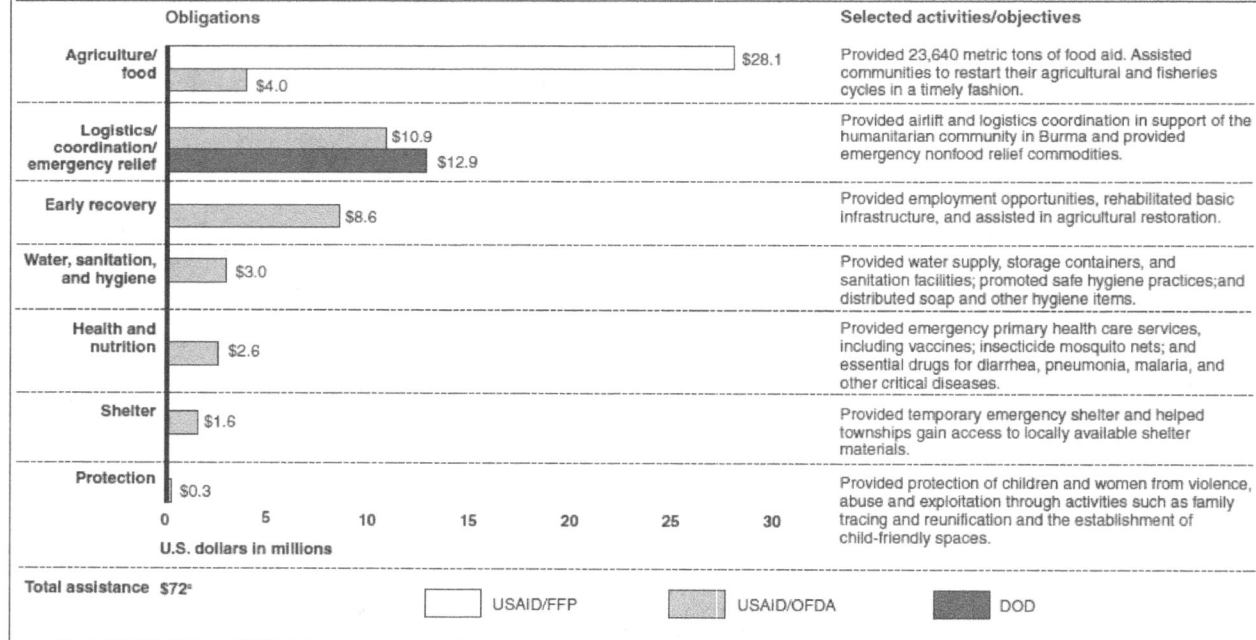

Emergency supplies provided by the U.S. government and other donors.

U.S. and Burmese military personnel off-load water and other critical supplies from U.S. C-130 aircraft.

Obligations

Sector	Value	Selected activities/objectives
Agriculture/ food	$28.1 / $4.0	Provided 23,640 metric tons of food aid. Assisted communities to restart their agricultural and fisheries cycles in a timely fashion.
Logistics/ coordination/ emergency relief	$10.9 / $12.9	Provided airlift and logistics coordination in support of the humanitarian community in Burma and provided emergency nonfood relief commodities.
Early recovery	$8.6	Provided employment opportunities, rehabilitated basic infrastructure, and assisted in agricultural restoration.
Water, sanitation, and hygiene	$3.0	Provided water supply, storage containers, and sanitation facilities; promoted safe hygiene practices;and distributed soap and other hygiene items.
Health and nutrition	$2.6	Provided emergency primary health care services, including vaccines; insecticide mosquito nets; and essential drugs for diarrhea, pneumonia, malaria, and other critical diseases.
Shelter	$1.6	Provided temporary emergency shelter and helped townships gain access to locally available shelter materials.
Protection	$0.3	Provided protection of children and women from violence, abuse and exploitation through activities such as family tracing and reunification and the establishment of child-friendly spaces.

U.S. dollars in millions

0   5   10   15   20   25   30

Total assistance $72[a]

☐ USAID/FFP   ☐ USAID/OFDA   ☐ DOD

Sources: GAO analysis of USAID and DOD data. Photos from DOD.

[a]Total does not include $2.9 million in USAID/OFDA support costs.

USAID/OFDA obligated the nearly $34 million as follows:

- $21.5 million was provided through 21 awards in 2008 to 20 different NGOs and UN organizations. Most of the awards were for emergency shelters, relief commodities and hygiene and sanitation facilities, including providing the means to access safe drinking water. Some awards also helped support capacity building for the local communities, particularly for food production.

- $5 million was provided in 2009 through seven awards to seven NGOs and UN organizations. These awards were largely modifications to the 2008 awards that extended the original grant time periods and provided extra funding for ongoing activities.

- $4.5 million was provided to procure and distribute relief commodities to various NGOs for distribution throughout the delta region in the early weeks following the cyclone.

- $2.9 million was provided for administrative, travel, and logistical support for the emergency response. This included travel and transportation costs for the disaster assistance response team members.

In addition to USAID/OFDA, USAID's Office of Food for Peace obligated $28.1 million of Food for Peace emergency food assistance[22] between September 2008 and January 2009, which WFP distributed to affected populations. The 23,640 metric tons of assistance included beans, rice, vegetable oil, and corn-soy blend. The first U.S. food shipment, consisting of 300 metric tons of corn-soy blend, arrived in Burma in September 2008 from U.S. prepositioned food stocks in Djibouti, Africa. Most of the other food supplies arrived from the United States between November 2008

---

[22]Section 3001 of Pub L. No. 110-246, the Food, Conservation, and Energy Act of 2008, changed the title of the underlying legislation from the Agricultural Trade Development Assistance Act of 1954, also known as P.L. 480, to the Food for Peace Act. Title II of the Food for Peace Act, administered by USAID, addresses donation of agricultural commodities for humanitarian purposes. (Other U.S. food aid programs are administered through the U.S. Department of Agriculture, including Food for Peace Title I, Food for Progress, and the McGovern-Dole International Food for Education and Child Nutrition programs.) U.S. commodities provided under Title II of the Food for Peace Act to meet emergency needs are generally distr buted through the World Food Program and nongovernmental organizations.

and January 2009, approximately 7 to 9 months after Cyclone Nargis struck Burma.[23]

DOD Transported Emergency Supplies and Assistance

DOD provided $12.9 million in transportation assistance and emergency supplies after Cyclone Nargis struck Burma. Between May 12 and June 22, 2008, DOD operated a U.S. government air-bridge with C-130 aircraft between Thailand and Burma and provided critical supplies, such as water, food, and emergency shelter material. The U.S. government air-bridge completed 185 airlifts and delivered more than $4 million of USAID/OFDA emergency relief supplies and commodities from DOD, UN agencies, NGOs, and the Government of Thailand. Upon the insistence of the Government of Burma, and because of a lack of other viable options, DOD provided early shipments of supplies to the Government of Burma for delivery. Soon thereafter, DOD consigned all emergency supplies flown to USAID's NGO partners.[24]

---

[23]The WFP Country Director in Burma during the humanitarian crisis said that Food for Peace's 4-month delay in delivering rice had a significant impact on WFP's ability to plan distr bution. We previously reported that multiple challenges affect the timeliness of U.S. food assistance delivery, including uncertain funding and inadequate planning, ocean transportation contracting practices, legal requirements, and inadequate coordination to systematically track and respond to delivery problems. Delivering U.S. food aid from vendor to village requires on average 4 to 6 months. We reported that while agencies have in some cases tried to expedite food aid delivery, the entire logistics process often lacks the timeliness required to meet humanitarian needs in emergencies. See GAO, *Foreign Assistance: Various Challenges Impede the Efficiency and Effectiveness of U.S. Food Aid*, GAO-07-560 (Washington, D.C.: Apr. 13, 2007). Also see GAO, *International Food Assistance: Better Nutrition and Quality Control Can Further Improve U.S. Food Aid*, GAO-11-491 (Washington, D.C.: May 12, 2011).

[24]When Cyclone Nargis struck Burma on May 2, 2008, the U.S. Pacific Command was conducting a major sea-based military exercise in the region, which included a disaster response component. As such, DOD was prepared to provide additional assistance if asked to do so. However, the Burmese government did not give DOD permission to conduct any relief operations beyond an air-bridge from Thailand.

U.S. Recovery Assistance Targets Four Sectors

To sustain the efforts initiated in the immediate aftermath of Cyclone Nargis, USAID's Regional Development Mission for Asia (USAID/RDMA) obligated an additional $9.7 million to fund four cooperative agreements in the priority sectors of livelihoods; health; water, sanitation, and hygiene; and shelter starting in May 2010, as shown in figure 5.[25] This assistance was targeted to provide for critical needs in sectors that required continued support as assistance moved into the recovery and reconstruction phases. USAID said its programs complemented other ongoing donor-funded programs, involved high levels of community participation, and fostered local beneficiary ownership. Ultimately, USAID will have supported relief and recovery in the Cyclone Nargis-affected communities for 4.5 years after the disaster at the close of these agreements.[26]

---

[25]USAID does not have a mission in Burma; therefore programs related to Burma are carried out by USAID/RDMA, headquartered in Bangkok, Thailand.

[26]The current USAID/RDMA cooperative agreements for Cyclone Nargis related assistance programs continue through December 31, 2012.

Figure 5: USAID/RDMA Early Recovery Assistance, Fiscal Years 2010 through 2013

USAID-funded bridge replacement.

USAID-funded maternal health care assistance.

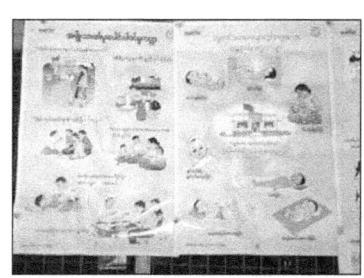

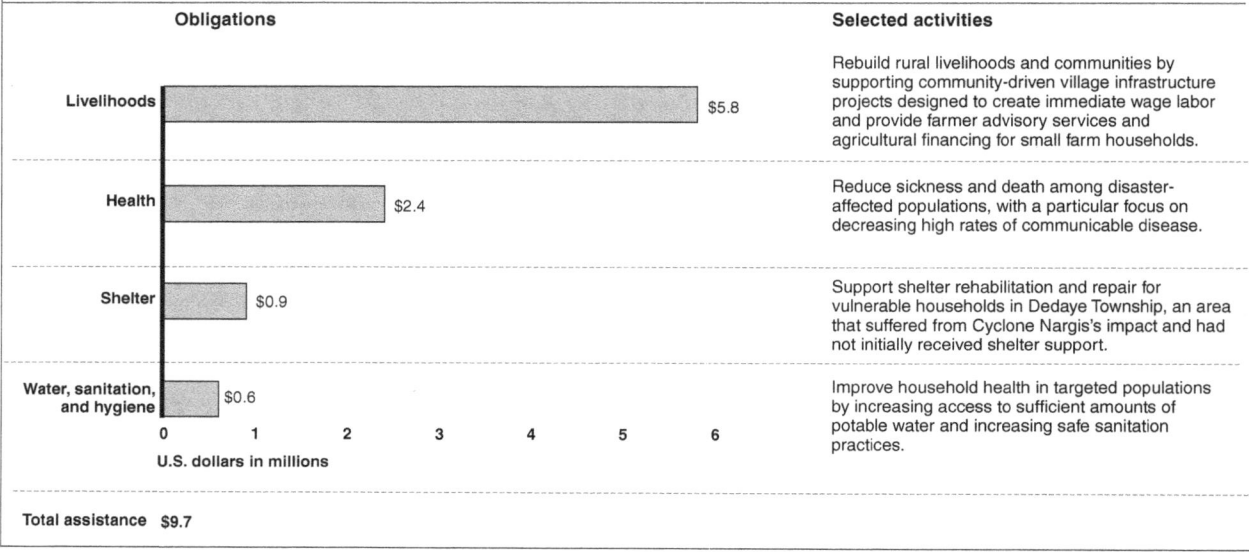

Obligations

Category	Obligations ($ millions)
Livelihoods	$5.8
Health	$2.4
Shelter	$0.9
Water, sanitation, and hygiene	$0.6

U.S. dollars in millions

Selected activities

Rebuild rural livelihoods and communities by supporting community-driven village infrastructure projects designed to create immediate wage labor and provide farmer advisory services and agricultural financing for small farm households.

Reduce sickness and death among disaster-affected populations, with a particular focus on decreasing high rates of communicable disease.

Support shelter rehabilitation and repair for vulnerable households in Dedaye Township, an area that suffered from Cyclone Nargis's impact and had not initially received shelter support.

Improve household health in targeted populations by increasing access to sufficient amounts of potable water and increasing safe sanitation practices.

Total assistance $9.7

Sources: GAO analysis of USAID data. Photos from GAO.

USAID Has Taken Actions to Help Ensure Funds Have Been Used As Intended, but Has Some Monitoring Weaknesses

USAID Took Actions Prior to Delivery of Assistance

Prior to delivery of assistance, USAID took several actions to help ensure that funds were used as intended and did not benefit sanctioned entities. First, USAID selected grantees that had experience working in Burma and with the United States. To provide immediate emergency assistance, USAID/OFDA generally selected grantees already working in Burma who were also familiar with USAID regulations and restrictions. In addition, USAID/OFDA said that they required all grantees, or their sub-grantees, to be registered to work in Burma before grants were finalized. This ensured grantees were able to begin providing assistance immediately. In providing follow-on assistance, USAID/RDMA decided to provide recovery funds to organizations that had received USAID/OFDA grants, a strategy that they said allowed them to implement their programs faster. They said these organizations had built relationships with the affected villages, were familiar with all the U.S. restrictions, and had demonstrated success operating in Burma. Officials reviewed the previous performance of each grantee in selecting organizations for the follow-on assistance.

Second, USAID/OFDA, State, and DOD officials initially decided to provide only low-value emergency relief supplies to limit the risk of theft by the Burmese military. Given that the Government of Burma insisted on receiving and distributing all aid in the initial days of the response, U.S. agencies said they chose their mix of relief supplies carefully to limit the risk of diversion by the Government of Burma. A State official told us that they chose certain goods, such as bottles of water and plastic sheeting, specifically with this purpose in mind. This official stated that the Government of Burma requested items such as helicopters and vehicles that could have been diverted, which the U.S. government did not provide.

Third, USAID/RDMA included written guidance in its agreements to emphasize restrictions and help grantees determine who in Burma is restricted from receiving U.S. assistance. For example, each agreement contains a clause clarifying that assistance cannot be provided to or through the Government of Burma, while recognizing that situations may arise where government workers, such as teachers or local health officials, may observe USAID-funded training. U.S. officials told us that they provide this extra guidance to help organizations better understand the restrictions. USAID/RDMA has also tried to design its programs to reduce the risks that U.S. assistance will benefit Government of Burma employees. For example, since U.S. funds generally cannot be used to provide any benefit to official village midwives because they are Government of Burma employees, USAID/RDMA approved grantees to work with community health workers, who are not government employees, as part of their health sector programs. In addition to the guidance in the agreements, USAID conducted post-award briefings with all partners to discuss the terms of the agreements, with an emphasis on ensuring that U.S. assistance does not benefit sanctioned entities. A USAID legal advisor participated in these briefings to answer participants' questions about how to differentiate between beneficiaries and local government employees.[27]

Finally, USAID obtained licenses from OFAC, or ensured its grantees had valid licenses, which allowed grantees to conduct all operations—including financial transactions—necessary to implement humanitarian assistance programs in Burma without violating U.S. sanctions.[28] USAID ensured that all of its grant agreements included copies of OFAC licenses. Under the terms of the licenses, USAID and its grantees had to continue to ensure that U.S. funding did not benefit sanctioned entities in Burma.

---

[27]USAID/RDMA officials also reported halting a number of activities leading up to the November 2010 elections to avoid the appearance of supporting the Burmese government in any manner.

[28]OFAC issued several renewals to USAID and State's specific license, which allows U.S. government grantees in Burma to transfer funds that are in direct support of conducting activities defined and authorized by their U.S. government grants and contracts. The license does not authorize the transfer of any blocked property that is not expressly authorized in the terms of the license.

| USAID Monitored Assistance Under Difficult Conditions, But Documentation Is Insufficient | Amid numerous travel and operational constraints, USAID has taken actions to monitor grantees' program delivery; however, we found that their site visits were not always documented as required.[29] USAID does not have an official presence in Burma, so staff must request permission to enter Burma weeks prior to any planned monitoring site visits; however, the Burmese government often does not grant permission in a timely manner, according to USAID officials. In addition, the Government of Burma placed numerous and significant restrictions on international travel to the affected region, which USAID officials said negatively affected their ability to conduct monitoring. USAID/OFDA officials also reported difficulties in conducting monitoring due to staffing constraints. They stated that a disaster of this magnitude could warrant fifteen to twenty members on the response team. However due to the inability to get visas for all team members, there were only four members in Burma during the height of the emergency response, and ultimately only seven team members gained access to Burma. USAID's ability to monitor is also constrained by the remoteness of the cyclone-affected areas. For example, one USAID grantee runs programs that are located on Middle Island, which took us 16 hours of travel by car and boat to reach under good conditions from Rangoon, where the U.S. embassy is located. |

As discussed below, despite the numerous constraints, USAID conducted some monitoring of its programs:

- *Emergency assistance.* USAID and State officials told us they monitored emergency assistance from May 2008 through May 2009. USAID/OFDA officials reported that members of USAID's disaster assistance response team made visits to the cyclone-hit delta region to oversee implementation of USAID-funded grant activities and to discuss results with beneficiaries from May 2008 to July 2008. However, the USAID-provided documentation of visits during this time focuses on the assessment of needs in the region, with no detailed discussion of monitoring of USAID programs. Further, USAID assigned an emergency disaster response coordinator—who was stationed in Burma from September 2008 to May 2009—to monitor

---

[29]USAID policy requires that the agreement officer or agreement officer's technical representative write a brief report highlighting his or her findings from site visits and include a copy of the report in the official award file. See USAID Automated Directives System (ADS) 303.3.17(b).

program activities.[30] She told us that during her time in Burma, she made only one monitoring site visit to each partner because of Burmese government-imposed travel restrictions. While she did not prepare formal trip reports, she told us that she reported her activities to USAID/OFDA staff members through e-mails and conversations and also reported her activities and findings to embassy staff for inclusion in classified cables issued by the embassy. However, while she was sometimes asked to clear information on the cables, she reported that she never saw finalized cables containing information she submitted.

- *Food aid.* To oversee USAID's food aid contributions to Burma, USAID assigned a food aid official to the disaster assistance response team in Bangkok roughly 2 weeks after Cyclone Nargis hit Burma. However, the food aid official returned to Washington, D.C., when she was unable to obtain a visa and monitored food aid activities from there, relying on disaster assistance response team members, other embassy officials, and WFP staff in Burma to monitor food assistance in a limited capacity. The official said she had regular informal communication via e-mail and telephone with WFP staff in Washington, D.C., and Burma. She was able to travel to Burma several months later, in September 2008, during which time she conducted site visits with WFP personnel across the Irrawaddy Delta. Her site visits included observations of food distributions and an inspection of a WFP warehouse. Upon returning, she drafted a trip report that was circulated within USAID, but was never finalized. The report included, among other things, her observations from the field visits and challenges encountered in the response.

- *Recovery assistance.* To monitor recovery assistance, USAID officials visited cyclone-affected areas three times between 2010 and 2011 and made several other visits to Rangoon, where they met with grantees. USAID officials said that while the Burmese government typically grants access, the level of uncertainty surrounding when they will grant the access makes it difficult to monitor aid delivery on short-term notice, limits the number of site visits they make, and precludes them from properly planning monitoring visits. USAID officials responsible for monitoring recovery assistance provided us with nine

---

[30]USAID also reported that a USAID officer from the Office of Transitions Initiatives conducted some site visits during the time between the departure of the disaster assistance response team and the arrival of the response coordinator.

trip reports, including two for trips to monitor grantee activities. The trip reports include headings for information such as activities monitored, key meetings, issues identified, recommendations, and photographs from site visits. We found that one of the two reports was generally lacking in detail. For example, the report included no detail on what the officials actually observed during the visit or any discussion of the activities they monitored in terms of potential issues or progress.

USAID staff reported that State officials from the embassy in Rangoon also conducted some monitoring activities; however, they did not receive instructions on monitoring procedures. According to a USAID official, State officials provided additional support for USAID staff on some site visits, or if traveling in the vicinity of USAID programs, they were asked to observe some of the activities and report back to USAID. While this monitoring was helpful, a USAID official told us that these State officials had not received formal USAID training on what to look for during site visits or how to conduct effective monitoring visits. All USAID agreement officers and their technical representatives are required to attend mandatory training that includes monitoring procedures.

USAID's Monitoring Includes Limited Financial Oversight and Relies on External Audits, but Staff Were Not Aware of Relevant Audit Findings

USAID's monitoring activities, including their limited number of site visits, involve little financial oversight, which is to help ensure funds are used as intended. USAID monitoring consists of program and financial monitoring. Program monitoring is focused on the effectiveness of USAID programs and is carried out by field officers, program officers, and the relevant agreement officer's technical representative (AOTR).[31] Financial monitoring is carried out by the AOTR and the relevant mission's office of financial management. For financial monitoring, USAID primarily relies on its reviews of grantee's quarterly self-reported cumulative expenditure

---

[31]The cognizant agreement officer designates a technical representative (AOTR) for each USAID agreement. The AOTR is responsible for ensuring that USAID exercises prudent management over its awarded assistance and makes the achievement of program objectives easier by monitoring and evaluating the recipient and its performance during the award. The AOTR's monitoring responsibilities include both financial and programmatic aspects.

data, and the grantee's annual single audit[32] to reveal any instances of financial noncompliance.

Grantee Financial Reports and Site Visits

Grantees are required to submit regular financial reports that are reviewed by the program office and the mission's office of financial management. These reports include cumulative financial transactions, such as drawdowns and expenditures. The office of financial management and the AOTR review these reports to assess the reasonableness of grantee drawdowns. USAID does not require grantees to provide supporting documentation, such as invoices or detailed transactions.[33] An official in USAID/RDMA's office of financial management told us that the AOTR, who is also the relevant program officer, compares these reports to information obtained from site visits and progress reports to ensure the information grantees report is reasonable.

USAID officials said that staff conducting monitoring in Burma, including the relevant AOTR, focused their site visits on programmatic issues but did not review grantee internal control frameworks or review disbursements to determine whether funds were used for intended purposes. However, USAID officials told us they consider their observation of grantees' use of materials procured with grant funds and the connection of those materials to the program activities described in the grant agreement to be a review of grantee financial actions. A USAID contracting officer reported that, given the limited amount of time the

---

[32]The Single Audit Act (31 U.S.C. §§ 7501-7507), as implemented by Office of Management and Budget guidance, requires each reporting entity (states, local governments, and nonprofit organizations) that expends $500,000 or more in federal awards in a fiscal year under multiple federal programs to obtain an annual "single audit." A single audit consists of (1) an audit and opinions on the fair presentation of the financial statements and the schedule of Expenditures of Federal Awards; (2) an understanding of and testing of internal control over financial reporting and the entity's compliance with laws, regulations, and contract or grant provisions that have a direct and material effect on certain federal programs (i.e., the program requirements); and (3) an audit and an opinion on compliance with applicable program requirements for certain federal programs.

[33]USAID regulations, which implement Office of Management and Budget Circular No. A-110's guidance on grant administration, do not require grantees to submit supporting documentation for expenditures. It does require grantees to retain, and make available for audits and examinations, financial records, supporting documents, statistical records, and all other records pertinent to an award, and to do so generally for a period of three years from the date of submission of the final expenditure report. See USAID grant regulations, 22 C.F.R. § 226.53 (Retention and Acceess Requirements for Records).

AOTR spends in the field monitoring, the emphasis is often on the programmatic side of her monitoring responsibilities. Further, the AOTR stated that the administrative burden associated with obtaining permission to enter Burma and travel to grantee sites detracts from USAID's ability to monitor the Cyclone Nargis-related programs more closely and make more meaningful assessments.

Single Audit Reports

USAID officials also told us they rely on the grantees' annual single audits, in addition to their review of grantee financial reports, to monitor compliance with their grant agreements; however, we found that relevant USAID program staff were not aware of some internal control weaknesses and questioned costs included in a grantee's single audit report.[34] Two of the three grantees we reviewed were required to submit single audits, and one had significant findings. We reviewed the June 30, 2009, and June 30, 2010, single audits of one of the grantees and the December 31, 2009, single audit of a second grantee. We found that the June 30, 2009, single audit of the first grantee had 11 findings related to internal controls and compliance with federal program requirements. For example, the auditors questioned cash payments to Burmese villages totaling $641,695 because the grantee did not provide the auditor with sufficient documentation for the cash payments. Officials from the grantee's Bangkok office told us that they addressed the auditor's findings and that they now maintain records of cash payments made to beneficiaries. We reviewed the same grantee's June 30, 2010, single audit report and noted that 9 of the 11 prior year findings related to the grantee's programs in Burma had been resolved, and the grantee is taking steps to resolve the remaining two findings.

During our fieldwork, USAID program officials responsible for overseeing the Burma programs said that they were not aware of the single audit findings. USAID officials told us that the USAID Inspector General's office reviews the single audit reports and distributes the audit packages to the

---

[34]We have raised concerns in the past about the quality of single audits and have testified that audits are not being conducted in accordance with professional standards and requirements. These audits may provide a false sense of assurance and could mislead users of the single audit reports. We also recommended that the Office of Management and Budget monitor the risk, cost-benefit, and efficiency and effectiveness of the single audit process. See GAO, *Single Audit Quality: Actions Needed to Address Persistent Audit Quality Problems*, GAO-08-213T (Washington, D.C.: Oct. 25, 2007) and *Single Audit: Opportunities Exist to Improve the Single Audit Process and Oversight*, GAO-09-307R (Washington, D.C.: Mar. 13, 2009).

relevant program offices. In this instance, because the Bangkok program staff did not receive any information from the Inspector General's office, they assumed that the single audits did not contain any findings related to the programs in Burma. USAID/RDMA officials told us that they would also have expected to uncover any audit findings during their preaward survey conducted in March 2010; however, the 2009 audit that contained the relevant findings for the first grantee was not released until a month after USAID's request for audits, and the grantee did not forward the report when it was released.[35] USAID/RDMA officials stated that if they had been informed of the single audit findings, they most likely would have awarded the grant to the NGO, but they would also have requested information from the grantee about how they were addressing the audit findings.

Questionable Costs for International Travel

In conducting a limited transaction review of selected USAID grantees, we found that two of the three grantees incurred questionable costs because they failed to obtain USAID's mandatory prior approval for each international trip funded by the grants.[36] According to USAID regulations, the grantees may only charge international travel costs to the award when USAID has previously approved each separate international trip for which such costs are incurred.[37] Under USAID regulations, prior approval means securing USAID's permission in advance of incurring costs on restricted items, and such advance permission may be obtained by specifying items in an approved budget.[38] According to USAID guidance,

---

[35]RDMA officials notified us that they received, in April 2011, a copy of the grantee's June 30, 2009, audit in response to their request.

[36]For our review, we selected three grantees that, in total, were awarded approximately $17.3 million (about 66 percent of total aid to NGOs from the United States), and conducted a limited review of the internal controls of the disbursement process. We reviewed supporting documentation for selected grantee expenditures; our work was not designed to identify all questionable costs or to estimate their extent.

[37]22 C.F.R. § 226.27, incorporating by reference the allowable costs provisions promulgated in the Office of Management and Budget Circular No. A-122, *Cost Principles for Non-Profit Organizations, codified at* 2 C.F.R. part 230, Appendix B (Selected Items of Cost), ¶ 51.E. (Foreign Travel Costs).

[38]22 C.F.R. § 226.27, incorporating by reference provisions in the Office of Management and Budget Circular No. A-122, *Cost Principles for Non-Profit Organizations, codified at* 2 C.F.R. § 230.25(b), which establishes a defined term for "prior approval."

"[f]ailure to comply with prior approval requirements generally causes USAID to deem the costs unallowable."[39]

Although the USAID award agreements require grantees to obtain prior approval for international travel, we found that this was not always done. For example, we found that for one grantee who has completed a $4.9 million grant, USAID had approved one traveler for six international trips between Thailand and Burma. However, this grantee incurred costs for 15 trips in 2008—10 trips between Thailand and Burma and 5 trips between Thailand and other countries, including Pakistan and Japan—at a total cost of about $7,357. A grantee official told us that they did not seek USAID prior approval for the additional trips, but that they did subsequently inform USAID of the trips in their required periodic reports. For another grantee, although the USAID agreement did not authorize any international travel, a grantee official told us that four international trips totaling approximately $3,633 had been paid for under their ongoing USAID award.

USAID officials told us that their practice is to review written requests that grantees submit for international travel and to grant approval if the work and travel proposed are to be performed in conformance with the award terms and sufficient funds are available. They also said that unplanned international travel can arise as a legitimate need for grantees in Burma due to the challenges in obtaining visas for non-Burmese staff. With regard to the international trips taken by the two grantees mentioned above, USAID/OFDA officials told us that they rely on some monitoring by the program staff and annual audits to detect unapproved travel; however, they said they did not approve the first grantee's international trips we questioned. Under USAID regulations on grant administration, USAID retains the right to recover funds from its grantees for any costs charged to the grant that a final USAID audit determines to be disallowed costs.[40] USAID/RDMA officials told us that for the second grantee, USAID approval for international trips was not necessary because they were within the budget limitations specified in the agreement for travel and transportation. However, we reviewed the agreement, noting that the travel and transportation budget is approximately $137,000; however, the

---

[39]USAID ADS 303.3.18(b).

[40]See USAID regulations (22 C.F.R. § 226.71(g)), which implement Office of Management and Budget Circular No. A-110's guidance on grant administration.

agreement did not expressly specify any international travel. Therefore compliance with existing regulations, guidance, and the USAID award agreement would require USAID's prior approval for each separate international trip. This grantee did not obtain such prior approval, and therefore incurred questionable costs that may be unallowable under its agreement.[41] In this grantee's agreement USAID reserved the right to an earlier recovery of unallowable costs, which includes requiring the grantee to refund the disallowed amount during the grant's performance period. Additionally, USAID policy provides that in certain circumstances USAID may ratify the grantee's activities by approving the disallowed international travel expenditures after the travel has occurred and the costs have been incurred.[42]

USAID Relies on Partners' Monitoring and Reporting of Activities

Given the difficulties in traveling to USAID-funded project sites in Burma to conduct monitoring, USAID relies on its partners' monitoring of program activities and self-reporting to gauge program progress and to identify any issues for follow-up during their limited number of site visits.[43] USAID told us that both the UN and NGO partners had established operations in the cyclone-affected region and had procedures for monitoring assistance. The UN agencies we reviewed told us that they had established a presence in the delta and conducted monitoring visits using Burmese local staff, supplemented by international staff site visits,

---

[41]USAID policy states that grantees must comply with prior approval requirements that are established in the grant agreement and that noncompliance with prior approval requirements generally causes USAID to deem the costs unallowable. See ADS 303.3.18(b) (Expenditures Requiring Prior Approval).

[42]USAID policy states that when it is in the best interest of the federal government and funds are available, the agreement officer (AO) may review the facts and circumstances of the expenditure made without prior approval and approve the expense if the: (1) expenditures are otherwise allocable, allowable, and reasonable; (2) AO could have approved the expenditures at the time that they were made; (3) AO has the authority to approve the same type of expenditure at the time of the request for approval; (4) approval promotes efficient implementation of USAID's program; or (5) facts and circumstances of the expenditure show that the grantee was not grossly negligent and did not intend to circumvent USAID requirements. USAID policy further states that the grantee must submit a written request to the AO addressing the criteria set out above and the AO must make a written determination. See ADS 303.3.18(b) (Expenditures Requiring Prior Approval).

[43]We did not evaluate the effectiveness of USAID grantees' monitoring activities for this report.

as feasible. In addition, the UN agencies are subject to internal audits on a regular basis. For example:

- WFP relied on both its existing oversight mechanisms as well as international organizations' staff present in the delta prior to Cyclone Nargis to carry out monitoring and oversight of its operations. According to a WFP official, these mechanisms helped the agency account for the purchase of commodities, their transport to established warehouses, and their distribution to implementing partners for distribution to affected communities.

- UNICEF set up five hubs throughout the delta region responsible for monitoring and oversight. In addition, UNICEF headquarters has an office of internal audit that audits each country office on a regular basis. The September 2009 audit of UNICEF's Burma Country Office included all major areas related to operations and programs, including emergency funds. The audit did not find any problems in the way UNICEF conducts its business in Burma.

- UNDP reported that all of its projects were implemented at the village level, with direct implementation and supervision by UNDP project personnel and by NGOs with direct UNDP supervision. In addition, an Independent Assessment Mission is organized annually to verify UNDP compliance with its mandate in Burma.[44] The three missions in 2008, 2009, and 2010 concluded that UNDP's program fully complied with the mandate. In addition, UNDP has provided written assurance to State each year to certify its compliance with the following U.S. conditions: (1) UNDP's work must focus on eliminating human suffering and addressing the needs of the poor, while providing no benefit to the Government of Burma, and (2) UNDP's work must be undertaken only through internal or international private voluntary organizations independent of the Government of Burma and in consultation with stakeholders, including the leadership of the National League for Democracy and National Coalition Government of the Union of Burma.

---

[44]UNDP works in Burma under a mandate from its executive board that focuses activities at programs with grassroots level impact in the areas of basic health, training and education, HIV/AIDS, the environment, and food security. As such, UNDP in Burma does not work with the Burmese government or its technical line departments, in terms of capacity building, training, or transfer of financial resources.

USAID also reported that NGOs established local offices in the delta region to oversee operations, conducting site visits with local and international staff. During our site visits with three implementing partners, we observed field-level internal controls, which are designed to safeguard funds. For example, several NGOs had cash transfer programs. To address the risk that individuals could steal or misuse funds, the organizations developed systems for documenting cash receipts and disbursements and for ensuring physical control over funds. For example, as illustrated in figure 6, one village we visited safeguarded cash by establishing lock boxes that required four assigned villagers be present to open—three key holders and the village president. Similar processes for documenting cash receipts and disbursements and ensuring physical controls were also utilized by other partners we examined. In addition, each implementing partner used methods to encourage local oversight by beneficiaries, such as forming local committees to make important resource allocation decisions and distributing transparency flyers to advertise the amount and recipients of delivered aid. In addition, one partner hired young female villagers as bookkeepers because, according to program officials, in this culture, Burmese villagers would more likely be willing to ask young females questions, as opposed to older males. Bookkeepers in two villages told us they had received several inquiries into the bookkeeping and expenditures from fellow villagers.

Figure 6: Observations of Field-Level Internal Controls

Observations of field level controls

Based on our observations, field level internal controls of one subgrantee in Middle Island have been designed and implemented to safeguard USAID funds. The subgrantee provides low interest micro-loans to qualified Burmese villagers who are in need of costly emergency medical care. The village's bookkeeper maintains detailed records to track loans made and repaid. And the village's president maintains physical custody of the iron box that holds the cash and records used for the micro-loans. There are three keyed locks on the box and three villagers each have possession of one of the three keys. The three villagers and the village president must be present to unlock the box. Having multiple people present when handling cash decreases the risk of misappropriation. We observed similar controls in other villages we visited.

Iron box that is used to store cash and records for the micro-loan program in Middle Island.

This is an image of the cash and records that are maintained in the iron box.

This photograph is of the village's record-keeping books, which are used to track micro-loans made and repaid.

Sources: GAO.

USAID has also relied on UN and NGO partners' required reports and informal communication to monitor progress and keep informed of issues. USAID required most NGO grantees to formally report to USAID quarterly, with some required to report semiannually.[45] USAID requires UN partners to report based on standard guidelines in ADS for awards to public international organizations.[46]

USAID/OFDA and USAID/RDMA officials also communicated informally with grantees in Bangkok and Rangoon. Even with this communication and reporting, we found that USAID program staff still observed issues requiring follow-up during the site visit to one grantee, reinforcing the importance of USAID site visits. During our site visit, USAID staff expressed concern about the way the grantee reported program results and the possibility that the reports may not be fully accurate because the local manager may be reluctant to raise issues or problems, given the Burmese cultural norms which discourage providing negative information. USAID staff told us that they will discuss this with the grantee and possibly revise the information the grantee reports to help ensure problems are identified.

U.S. and Other Organizations Found No Evidence of Misuse

USAID, State, UN, and international NGO officials said they examined all reports of potential misuse of assistance within their programs and found no evidence of misuse, although they did find that some beneficiaries sold small amounts of materials. For example, a USAID official told us that a beneficiary may sell an item, such as a USAID supplied tarp, he no longer needs in order to buy items that he does need. However, USAID officials told us this may not be a misuse of assistance as it still allows beneficiaries to obtain goods they need. USAID and DOD officials said

---

[45]USAID official told us the decision to require only semiannual reporting for some partners was directly related to the length of the program. For example, one agreement that stipulated semiannual reporting was a 1-year program, and the official did not want the grantee spending a disproportionate amount of time preparing progress reports as opposed to implementing the assistance.

[46]USAID ADS 308.3.14, which references the standard provisions for cost-type grants to public international organizations, requires a UN-specific audit and records clause to be included in all awards to the UN. The grantee must agree to furnish the U.S. government with a final report on activities carried out under the grant, including accounting for grant funds in sufficient detail to enable USAID to liquidate the grant. The report must be submitted to the U.S. Mission to the UN in New York, New York, for forwarding to the USAID program office.

they kept very detailed lists of all relief supplies provided. USAID said they gave these lists to U.S. Embassy staff who used them in market surveys. In these surveys, Embassy staff, including Burmese national staff, monitored local markets in the delta and Rangoon for evidence that U.S.-provided relief materials were being sold. USAID/OFDA officials also reported that branding USAID-donated goods was important for effectively monitoring assistance, as any diverted aid would be easily identifiable.

In a highly publicized example of potential diversion of assistance, WFP reported that during the first week of the Cyclone Nargis response, the Burmese government airport authorities briefly took control of the contents of two flights, including 38 tons of high energy biscuits, when they landed. However, these contents were released to WFP the next day after negotiations with the Ministry of Social Welfare.

Organizations Responding to Cyclone Nargis Experienced Similar Challenges and Developed Lessons Learned

Our analysis of 16 evaluative reports[47] from NGOs, governments, and UN agencies as well as interviews with U.S., UN, and NGO officials found that organizations responding to Cyclone Nargis experienced similar challenges in four main categories: access to affected populations, coordination among responding organizations, implementation of assistance, and in-country disaster response capacity. We also identified some lessons learned to confront these, and other, challenges from these organizations' experiences in responding to Cyclone Nargis. In analyzing the various challenges each organization reported facing in their response to Cyclone Nargis, we developed the four main categories, as well as several subcategories, to capture the similarities of challenges reported and quantify the number of times each type of challenge was reported. We then reviewed the lessons identified and selected those relevant to the overall categories and subcategories. Not all responding organizations faced the challenges reported or might find the lessons applicable.[48] (App. IV contains additional information on the challenges and lessons learned, and app. V discusses U.S.-specific challenges.)

---

[47]We reviewed 16 reports for lessons learned, and 15 of those same reports for experienced challenges. The reports were compiled by NGOs, UN agencies, a U.S. agency, and UN-led sector-based coordination groups, such as the Water, Sanitation, and Hygiene Cluster. (See app. I for information on our scope and methodology.)

[48]We did not assess the feasibility of implementing the lessons learned.

Restricted Access Delayed Response, Limited Coverage, and Complicated the Operating Environment

According to the reports we reviewed, restricted access and poor infrastructure delayed assistance, limited coverage, and complicated emergency response and recovery operations for some organizations in Burma (see fig. 7). The most frequently cited challenge regarding restricted access was obtaining travel authorizations from the Burmese government, both to enter Burma and to travel around the country. The Government of Burma initially restricted foreigners from entering into Burma and required government issued authorizations for international staff to travel within Burma. Consequently, the emergency relief and humanitarian efforts became highly dependent on Burmese nationals and international staff already in Burma. These responders were often overworked and operated beyond their mandate or outside their areas of expertise. In addition, responders faced poor roads and infrastructure and high transportation costs. Many areas were only accessible by boat or by air and, given the scarcity of boats, hiring them became very difficult and air drops were too expensive. The reports we reviewed suggest that similar access and infrastructure constraints call for creative approaches to negotiating with the host country government and looking for ways to modify normal operations, such as by bringing in national staff from other countries and owning boats as opposed to trying to hire them in a market experiencing shortages and inflated prices.

Figure 7: Access to Cyclone-Affected Populations, Common Challenges and Lessons Learned

COMMON CHALLENGES	LESSONS LEARNED
Restricted access delayed response activities, limited coverage, and complicated the overall operating environment.	Similar restricted situations call for creative negotiation approaches and flexible adaptation.
• Obtaining Government of Burma authorization to enter and operate in Burma delayed assistance and complicated logistics. (13)	• ASEAN and the Tripartite Core Group were successful in building trust with the Government of Burma and gaining access for international responders. • UNICEF brought in their Burmese staff from other country offices because they did not require entry visas and internal travel permits. • Alternative coordination methods can be used to better engage relevant organizations without putting them at risk. For example, UNICEF, the only organization with a formal agreement with the Ministry of Education to carry out emergency education activities, included other partners through the cluster system.
• Transportation obstacles further restricted access to affected populations. (8)	• Boats and helicopters helped to reach remote villages. Because hiring boats was difficult, one report suggests that buying boats or renting them by the month might be more effective.

Sources: GAO analysis of 16 reports on Cyclone Nargis response.

Note: We identified challenges and lessons learned independently of each other. The parenthetical number following the description of each challenge is the number of analyzed reports citing that challenge as a significant obstacle. Because lessons varied greatly across organizaions, we did not quantify the number of reports citing each lesson.

Complex and Poorly Managed Coordination Resulted in Disjointed Response Efforts

Our review found that coordination among donors was also problematic (see fig. 8). Difficulties in communicating between headquarters in either Bangkok or Rangoon and the field were the most commonly reported coordination challenge. As a result, occasionally decisions made at headquarters conflicted with those made in the field. Reports mentioned the physical distance between the locations and the limited, and unreliable, telecommunication services in the delta, as some of the reasons contributing to the communication challenges. Reliable internet access was generally lacking in the field, and the Burmese government restricted the importation and use of communications equipment. Another widely experienced challenge was gathering and sharing data among responding organizations. Many reports noted that shared information was often inaccurate, unreliable, and inconsistent. Some reports attributed this challenge to factors such as mistrust among organizations, poor information management practices of some groups, and a lack of commonly used and readily available reporting mechanisms or common databases accessible by all responding organizations. Lastly, USAID's after action report on the U.S. Cyclone Nargis Emergency Response cited a challenge within the U.S. government of carrying out a coordinated response. Conflicting agendas amongst USAID, DOD, and State officials resulted in coordination difficulties related to the appropriateness, timing, procurement, and distribution of aid. USAID officials reported that, while their response was based on humanitarian needs, State and DOD also had political motives which included engagement with the Burmese government.[49] As a result, USAID officials reported that DOD conducted air lifts for a longer period of time than some USAID officials thought was necessary, and in some cases provided aid that USAID considered inappropriate. The lessons we identified emphasize the need for installing common reporting formats for all organizations to use and improving support to the field offices, including providing more resources such as local information centers.

---

[49]In commenting on a draft of this report, DOD officials disagreed with USAID's assertion that DOD had political motives, stating their response was in support of overall U.S. humanitarian objectives.

Figure 8: Coordination between Responding Organizations, Common Challenges and Lessons Learned

COMMON CHALLENGES	LESSONS LEARNED
Complex and poorly managed coordination resulted in disjointed response efforts based on limited data on needs and coverage.	Improve coordination by using standard reporting and information-sharing forms and increasing support for field staff.
• Coordination between headquarters and provisional field offices was often disjointed. (12)	• Establish local resource centers and NGO liaison officers at field locations. Increase visits from Rangoon-based leadership.
• Complications in collecting and sharing information hindered assistance delivery. (10)	• The Myanmar Information Management Unit and cluster-managed resources were useful to information management. Expand responsibility of cluster information managers, including increased coordination with actors with similar roles, such as the OCHA reports officer.
• Coordination among international responders lacked coherence. (6)	• Predevelop common reporting templates and information management tools (accompanied by clear guidelines) to improve the consistency and reliability of shared information.

Sources: GAO analysis of 16 reports on Cyclone Nargis response.

Note: We identified challenges and lessons learned independently of each other. The parenthetical number following the description of each challenge is the number of analyzed reports citing that challenge as a significant obstacle. Because lessons varied greatly across organizations, we did not quantify the number of reports citing each lesson.

Some Decisions Based on Limited Information and Burma's Unique Constraints Hindered Implementation Effectiveness

The reports we reviewed highlighted implementation challenges, including the use of incompatible relief supplies, inappropriate targeting, and inability to monitor (see fig. 9). Many reports cited examples of donated or procured assistance supplies that were inferior in quality or incompatible with local conditions, which limited their usefulness. Examples included

- tents, which proved to be inappropriate given the delta's hot and humid conditions;

- 5-gallon water bottles, which were heavy and difficult to transport; and

- medical supplies that had instructions printed only in non-Burmese languages.

In addition, cultural norms and inadequate information about affected populations complicated responders' efforts to effectively target and distribute aid. For example, some organizations based targeting decisions on the level of need of individuals; however, Burmese culture values fairness and equality, and as a result many villages would redistribute supplies to ensure all villagers received something, thereby reducing the efficacy of the organizations' efforts to target the neediest with their aid.[50] Lastly, the lack of trained personnel in the field, the remoteness of certain locations, or lack of government approval hindered robust monitoring and evaluation mechanisms. Strategies reported to improve effectiveness of implementation included engaging with local beneficiaries to involve them in the development of procurement, targeting, and distribution strategies.

---

[50]We reported recently on a similar challenge experienced in the broader context of international food assistance. We found that targeting of international food assistance can often be undermined at the recipient level by the cultural practice of sharing in local communities. See GAO-11-491.

Figure 9: Implementation of Assistance, Common Challenges and Lessons Learned

COMMON CHALLENGES	LESSONS LEARNED
The restrictive operating environment and narrowly-informed approaches of responders hindered the effectiveness of some response activities.	Focusing more on local engagement and enhancing protection strategies could improve the effectiveness of response activities.
• Donated and procured goods were sometimes inferior or incompatible with local conditions. (10)	• One organization noted that a focus on traditional practices and local participation contributed to beneficiary satisfaction. • UNICEF balanced the speed and cost of aid delivery by importing goods only while local, low-cost solutions were being developed. • FAO suggests delegating procurement to implementing partners at the township level.

• Targeting and distribution of assistance were obstructed by political, logistical, or organizational capacity factors. (10)	• Targeting efforts should consider the Burmese tradition of equity that underlies redistribution within communities. FAO concluded that communities should decide how aid would be appropriately distributed.
	
	• Further strengthen protection mechanisms through:
	
	    • integrating cross-cutting protection, gender, and age issues;
	
	    • engaging the Department of Social Welfare; and
	
	    • establishing organizational responsibility at the onset of an emergency.
	
	• UNICEF found success with supporting community-based child protection groups.

• Monitoring, evaluation, and oversight mechanisms were limited. (3)	• Technical field consultants helped facilitate monitoring and oversight. Two reports advocated for community-level monitoring.

Sources: GAO analysis of 16 reports on Cyclone Nargis response.

Limited In-Country Preparedness and Capacity Exacerbated the Impact and Hindered Response Efforts

Our review found that limited emergency preparedness and response capacity in Burma exacerbated the impact of the disaster and hindered efforts throughout the response (see fig. 10). One of the most frequently cited capacity challenges was the inability to meet the high demand for technical, skilled, and experienced disaster responders. The number of staff in Burma experienced or trained in disaster relief was below what was needed. As a result, some positions had to be filled with personnel that had no previous experience and limited knowledge of humanitarian response principles, which caused delays or difficulties in carrying out the response. Also, many organizations described their interaction with local organizations in coordinated response activities as limited due to Burmese political, cultural, or capacity factors. These factors included language and cultural barriers, lack of access to electronically shared information, limited modes of transportation, and insufficient time and staff to attend coordination meetings. In addition, the response to Cyclone Nargis was hampered by weak early warning systems and disaster preparedness plans in Burma, as well as among international organizations. Lastly, emergency supply stocks and prepositioned food supplies were lacking within the country. Responders cited the improvement of in-country emergency preparedness and response capacity through personnel training and local engagement as critical.

Figure 10: In-Country Capacity, Common Challenges and Lessons Learned

COMMON CHALLENGES	LESSONS LEARNED
Limited in-country preparedness and response capacity exacerbated the impact of the disaster and hindered efforts throughout the response.	In-country preparedness and response capacity could be improved through personnel training and local engagement.
• Relatively inexperienced in-country personnel had difficulty meeting all response needs. (13)	• Cyclone Nargis highlighted the need for standby arrangements with skilled personnel who have emergency response experience. This should include a roster of local actors who receive capacity training that is refreshed and updated periodically over the long term.
• Local participation in coordinated response activities was limited. (7)	• During the response, national actors benefited from greater mobility and acceptance from government authorities and local communities. Strategies to further engage these actors include the following: • appointing local counterparts to coordination positions, • developing alternatives to electronic information sharing, and • translating coordination meetings and key documents into Burmese.
• Early warning systems and disaster preparedness plans were weak at all levels. (7)	• A database of in-country information technology and communications support, suppliers, warehousing, and transportation providers would be helpful. One organization told us that prepositioning relief supplies was essential and recommended establishing reserve warehouses in Southeast Asia.

Sources: GAO analysis of 16 reports on Cyclone Nargis response.

Note: We identified challenges and lessons learned independently of each other. The parenthetical number following the description of each challenge is the number of analyzed reports citing that challenge as a significant obstacle. Because lessons varied greatly across organizations, we did not quantify the number of reports citing each lesson.

Conclusions

In response to the urgent humanitarian needs in Burma resulting from Cyclone Nargis, the U.S. government has obligated about $85 million for emergency response and recovery activities under difficult conditions stemming from political concerns and operational constraints. USAID has taken actions to monitor its assistance and ensure funds have been used as intended and did not benefit sanctioned entities. Given USAID's limited ability to visit project sites in Burma, actions such as conducting more comprehensive financial oversight, documenting site visits, and communicating past audit findings become even more important to help ensure funds are used for intended purposes. The fact that single audit reports are issued several months after the end of an entity's fiscal year, further supports the need for current, on-going financial monitoring. Periodic reviews of grantee internal controls together with a review of some of the grantee's disbursement transactions and supporting documentation would strengthen USAID's financial oversight and help ensure compliance with the terms of the grant agreements, including compliance with international travel requirements. Reviewing questionable costs for international travel under the completed and ongoing grants could enable USAID to recover any costs that USAID determines to be unallowable. Documenting site visits, as required by USAID policy, provides a record that can be particularly useful when program staff change. By including relevant and sufficient detail, these documents create a historical record on which future monitoring and grant award decisions can be based. Finally, better communication of single audit findings among the USAID offices would ensure that program staff become aware of important issues they should pursue when monitoring assistance.

Recommendations for Executive Action

We recommend that the Administrator of USAID direct the appropriate mission and offices to improve management of grants related to Burma by taking actions, such as:

- enhancing financial monitoring of agreements by including periodic reviews of grantee internal controls, transactions, and disbursement records;

- providing grantees with specific guidance on the approval process for international travel requests, and ensuring that USAID staff monitor grantees' expenditures for compliance with related laws, regulations, and grant agreements, including international travel;

- reinforcing the requirement for staff to formally document site visits to grantees; and

- ensuring all relevant offices are made aware of audit findings in a timely manner.

We also recommend that the Administrator of USAID direct the appropriate mission and offices to follow-up on the questionable costs associated with international travel that we identified in this report and take action as appropriate on any identified unallowable costs.

Agency Comments and Our Evaluation

USAID and DOD provided written comments on a draft of this report. We have reprinted their comments in appendixes VI and VII. These agencies, along with the Departments of State and the Treasury and the UN Country Team in Burma, provided technical comments and updated information, which we have incorporated throughout this report, as appropriate.

USAID, the agency to which we directed our recommendations, concurred with our recommendations. USAID said that financial monitoring is critical and that financial reviews should be enhanced as allowable given regulatory and operational limitations. They also said that existing guidance in USAID awards should be adhered to and enforced and USAID's ability to conduct preawards surveys and timely audits should be enhanced. USAID also recognized the importance of documenting oversight while noting that in disaster response environments, the main focus is on life-saving and life-sustaining activities. USAID agreed that relevant offices and officials should be aware of adverse audit information given their monitoring responsibilities. USAID also agreed to conduct appropriate follow-up actions with the grantees on questionable costs associated with international travel that we identified. In addition, USAID commented on our characterization of their actions to ensure funds were used as intended, as well as the evidence that assistance had not been misused. We made changes consistent with the information we obtained.

We are sending copies of this report to interested members of Congress; the Administrator of USAID; the Secretaries of Defense, State, and the Treasury; the UN Country Team in Burma; and relevant NGOs. The report is also available at no charge on the GAO Web site at http://www.gao.gov.

If you or your staffs have any questions about this report, please contact me at (202) 512-9601 or melitot@gao.gov. Contact points for our Office of Congressional Relations and Public Affairs may be found on the last page of this report. GAO staff who made major contributions to this report are listed in appendix VI.

Thomas Melito
Director, International Affairs and Trade

Appendix I: Scope and Methodology

UN and U.S. Assistance

To describe assistance provided by UN and U.S. agencies in response to Cyclone Nargis, we reviewed documents, including grants, cooperative agreements, and progress reports, from UN agencies, the U.S. Agency for International Development (USAID), Department of Defense (DOD), Department of State (State), and nongovernmental organizations (NGO). We also interviewed United Nations (UN), U.S., and NGO officials in Washington, D.C.; Bangkok, Thailand; and Rangoon, Burma; and conducted site visits to select USAID-funded recovery projects in Burma.

The team obtained the data for UN agency assistance to Burma from the UN Office for the Coordination of Humanitarian Affairs (UN OCHA) Financial Tracking Service. We report UN agency obligations.[1] In assessing this data we found that the service data are reported by donors and appealing organizations. UN OCHA reported that they cross-check and reconcile the data to ensure there is no duplicate reporting of funding and to verify the accuracy of the numbers reported.

The tracking service makes efforts to collect and report all humanitarian assistance. However, the service guarantees only that suitable humanitarian funding information sent to it will be posted; it cannot guarantee that it will find and record information not sent to it. Given this limitation, it is possible that we may have underreported total assistance obligated through UN agencies. Overall, through our review of UN OCHA procedures for capturing and reporting the data, we found the data sufficiently reliable to report on obligations as compiled by UN OCHA.

We obtained data on U.S. obligations from USAID and DOD. For USAID obligations, we verified these data against the underlying agreements and found the data to be sufficiently reliable to report on total assistance obligated by the Office of Foreign Disaster Assistance, Regional Development Mission for Asia, and Food for Peace. For DOD obligations, we interviewed officials on their process for recording and reconciling expenses and found the total amount of assistance reported by DOD to be sufficiently reliable for our purposes.

---

[1]For purposes of this report, we are defining UN obligations to include all assistance outlined in a signed agreement, such as a contract, grant, or cooperative agreement. We did not include data on UN pledges.

Actions to Help Ensure Funds Were Used as Intended

To assess USAID actions to help ensure funds were used as intended and did not benefit sanctioned entities, we reviewed program and financial files for funds USAID awarded in response to Cyclone Nargis and spoke with USAID officials about their monitoring of programs. The documents we reviewed included grants and cooperative agreements awarded for Cyclone Nargis response activities, progress reports, and Department of the Treasury Office of Foreign Assets Control licenses. We also conducted a limited internal controls review of three NGOs, which collectively account for 66 percent of funding that USAID awarded to international NGOs to respond to Cyclone Nargis. We also met with officials from these three NGOs and with USAID officials responsible for financial oversight of the NGOs' programs.

In choosing the three NGOs to review, we selected those organizations that had ongoing recovery activities in response to Cyclone Nargis, in addition to having conducted emergency response and relief activities. This risk-based approach to grantee selection allowed us to examine the evolution of oversight by USAID from the immediate aftermath of Cyclone Nargis to the current recovery phase, more than 2 years later. The three organizations that met these criteria received multiple USAID awards beginning in 2008 to conduct emergency relief operations, such as distribution of commodities, as well as to conduct recovery work, such as rehabilitating markets and reconstructing sanitation facilities.

For our limited internal controls review of these three NGOs, we interviewed grantee officials, reviewed single audit reports; and performed detailed reviews of transactions. We also tested certain grantee expenditures. We reviewed supporting documentation for selected grantee expenditures for sufficiency, compliance with laws, regulations, and grant agreements, as well as appropriateness. While we identified some questionable expenditures, our work was not designed to identify all improper or questionable expenditures or to estimate their extent.

Challenges and Lessons Learned

To report on the challenges and lessons learned from the Cyclone Nargis emergency response, we reviewed relevant evaluative reports from U.S. government and UN agencies, and NGOs involved in the response. We selected 16 reports for content analysis based on their methodology.[2] Specifically, the reports needed to outline reasonable methods for collecting data—such as surveys and interviews with responders—and a process for filtering this information prior to reporting.[3]

The reports offer a range of scope and content. While some reports evaluate a specific organizational response, others include the efforts of and information from several organizations. Some reports focus on the early months of the response, while others evaluate efforts up to almost two years after the onset of the emergency. Table 1 lists the reports we included in our review.

Table 1: Reports Included in Our Review

Report
1   *Best Practices and Lessons Learnt: UNICEF Myanmar's Response following Cyclone Nargis* (Rangoon, Burma, April 2009)
2   *Evaluation of CARE Myanmar's Cyclone Nargis Response*, Ternstrom Consulting AB (Sweden, December 2008)
3   *IFRC, Emergency Shelter Cluster Review: Cyclone Nargis, Myanmar*, Jessica Alexander (Burma, April 2009)
4   *USAID, Cyclone Nargis Burma Humanitarian Response After Action Review Report* (Washington, D.C., September 2009)
5   *Evaluation of Christian Aid's Response to Cyclone Nargis*, Andrew Featherstone (United Kingdom, March 2009)
6   *SIDA-Funded OSRO/MYA/902/SWE Project Implemented by FAO in Myanmar: Interim Evaluation Report* (Rome, Italy, March 2010)
7   *Myanmar Inter-Agency Contingency Plan (IA-CP) Version 2.0, OCHA* (Rangoon, Burma, August 2010)
8   *Inter-Agency Real Time Evaluation of the Response to Cyclone Nargis*, UN (New York, NY, December 2008)

---

[2] We reviewed 16 reports for lessons learned, and 15 of those same reports for experienced challenges. The report excluded from the latter is a planning document with limited discussion of actual response efforts. Nevertheless, the document contains a "lessons learned" section, which is informative with respect to lessons.

[3] We contacted the authors of reports that did not include adequate detail on methodology and requested further information.

	Report
9	*Evaluation of the Save the Children Response to Cyclone Nargis,* Andrew Featherstone (Burma, April 2009)
10	*Cyclone Nargis: Lessons for Operational Agencies,* Ramalingam, B. and S. Pavanello, Active Learning Network for Accountability and Performance in Humanitarian Action (United Kingdom, May 2008)
11	*Inter-Agency Review of the Myanmar Protection of Children and Women Cluster Response to Cyclone Nargis* (Rangoon, Burma, October 2008)
12	*Review of the WASH Cluster in Myanmar, Following the Cyclone Nargis Response* (Rangoon, Burma, January 2009)
13	*ActionAID: Mid-Term Evaluation Emergency Response Programme* (Rangoon, Burma: July 2009)
14	*Review of FAO Implemented UN Central Emergency Response Fund (CERF) Projects: Country Case Study Report Myanmar* (May 2010)
15	*A Humanitarian Call: The ASEAN Response to Cyclone Nargis* (Jakarta, Indonesia, July 2010)
16	*UNICEF, Myanmar 2008 Consolidated Emergency Report* (Rangoon, Burma, March 2009)

Source: GAO.

Once we selected reports that met the above criteria, two analysts separately identified challenges and lessons learned cited within each document. We defined "challenge" as any significant obstacle that hindered a specific response effort. We defined "lesson learned" as any successful or promising approach derived from a Cyclone Nargis response that could enable actors to overcome challenges or improve efforts in future emergencies. Furthermore, a "lesson" must be derived from a common or well-proven response experience and address Burma's unique political, social, or environmental circumstances. After the two analysts independently identified reported challenges and lessons based on these criteria, they compared the results and reconciled inconsistencies. A supervisory analyst reviewed their work.

We also gathered information on challenges and lessons from interviews with the previously mentioned responding organizations. We used this input to substantiate data gained from the document review, as well as supplement it with information that was not previously reported. For reporting purposes, once all the challenges were identified, we tallied each under broad categories and subcategories that summarized the similarities amongst the various challenges being reported. These categories and subcategories were developed by us based on an analysis of the challenges identified as well as our experience from previous disaster assistance work. Similarly, we reviewed the lessons we identified from the various reports and selected relevant lessons that address the subcategories of challenges we identified. Not all responding organizations faced the challenges reported or might find the lessons applicable. We did not assess the feasibility of implementing the lessons learned.

We conducted this performance audit from July 2010 to July 2011 in accordance with generally accepted government auditing standards. Those standards require that we plan and perform the audit to obtain sufficient, appropriate evidence to provide a reasonable basis for our findings and conclusions based on our audit objectives. We believe that the evidence obtained provides a reasonable basis for our findings and conclusions based on our audit objectives.

Appendix II: Mission Descriptions of the UN Agencies That Responded to Cyclone Nargis

Table 2 describes the overall mission of each UN agency that provided aid after Cyclone Nargis, as depicted in figure 3.

Table 2: Mission Descriptions of the UN Agencies That Responded to Cyclone Nargis

Agency	Mission
World Food Program (WFP)	WFP's mission is to get food where it is needed in emergencies, and to use food to help communities rebuild after an emergency has passed. WFP also works to reduce chronic hunger and under-nutrition and to strengthen the capacity of countries to reduce hunger, among other activities.
United Nations Children's Fund (UNICEF)	UNICEF advocates for the protection of children's rights and helps meet children's basic needs. It responds in emergencies to relieve the suffering of children and those who provide their care, and it promotes the equal rights of women and girls and supports their full participation in developing their communities, among other activities.
United Nations Development Program (UNDP)	UNDP is the UN's global development network and helps developing countries attract and use aid effectively to address the challenges of democratic governance, poverty reduction, crisis prevention and recovery, environment and energy, and HIV/AIDS.
Food and Agriculture Organization of the United Nations (FAO)	FAO is the lead UN agency for agriculture, forestry, fisheries, and rural development. Its mission is to raise levels of nutrition and standards of living, to improve agricultural productivity, and to better the condition of rural populations.
United Nations High Commissioner for Refugees (UNHCR)	UNHCR's mission is to safeguard the rights and well-being of refugees and does this by leading and coordinating international efforts to protect refugees and resolve refugee problems.
World Health Organization (WHO)	WHO is responsible for providing leadership on global health matters, shaping the health research agenda, setting norms and standards, articulating evidence-based policy options, providing technical support to countries, and monitoring and assessing health trends.
Office for the Coordination of Humanitarian Affairs (UN OCHA)	UN OCHA is reponsible for bringing together humanitarian actors in response to an emergency to ensure a coherent response and a framework within which each actor can contribute effectively to the overall response effort.
International Labor Organization (ILO)	ILO's mission is to promote standards and fundamental rights and principles in the workplace, encourage decent employment opportunities, enhance social protection, and strengthen dialogue on work-related issues. Its mandate in Burma was more limited and was restricted to activities for the elimination of forced labor, including forced and/or underage recruitment and human trafficking, and for the introduction of freedom of association.
United Nations Population Fund (UNFPA)	UNFPA promotes health and equal opportunity for men, women, and children. It supports countries in using population data for policies and programs to reduce poverty, combat the spread of HIV, protect the dignity of women, and promote family planning and prenatal care.
United Nations Educational, Scientific, and Cultural Organization (UNESCO)	UNESCO's mission is to contribute to the building of peace, the eradication of poverty, sustainable development, and intercultural dialogue through education, the sciences, culture, communication, and information.
United Nations Human Settlements Program(UN-HABITAT)	UN-HABITAT's mission is to promote socially and environmentally sustainable towns and cities with the goal of providing adequate shelter for all.

Source: GAO analysis of UN data.

Appendix III: U.S. Emergency Assistance Provided to Burma in Response to Cyclone Nargis

The U.S. government funded emergency humanitarian assistance for townships in Burma damaged by Cyclone Nargis. As shown in figure 11, the townships of Bogale, Labutta, and Mawlamyinegyun received the most extensive range of assistance, covering at least five of the seven relief sectors the U.S. funded.

Figure 11: U.S. Government Assistance to Townships in Burma, by Location

	Bogale	Dala	Dedaye	Kawhmu	Kungyangon	Kyaiklat	Kyauktan	Labutta	Maubin	Mawlamyinegyun	Myaungmya	Ngapudaw[a]	Pathein	Pyapon	Pyinkhayine Island	Rangoon	Seikgyikanaunglo	Set San	Twantay
Agriculture and food security	●	●	●	●	●	●	●	●	●	●			●					●	
Early recovery	●	●	●	●	●	●	●	●	●	●	●		●	●				●	
Emergency relief supplies/logistics[a]	●	●	●	●	●		●		●	●	●	●	●	●	●	●	●		
Health							●				●								
Protection	●																		
Shelter and settlements	●						●		●										
Water, sanitation, and hygiene	●						●			●	●	●		●					

Source: GAO based on USAID 2008 map *USG Humanitarian Assistance to Burma.*

Note: Map does not include location of U.S.-funded food aid distributions. Map contains some townships that have the same name as villages.

[a]Ngapudaw is the only township that received logistics assistance.

Appendix IV: Organizations Responding to Cyclone Nargis Experienced Interconnected Challenges and Developed Lessons Learned

Our analysis of 16 evaluative reports[1] from NGOs, governments, and UN agencies found that organizations responding to Cyclone Nargis experienced interconnected challenges and developed lessons learned in four categories: access to affected populations, coordination among responding organizations, implementation of assistance, and in-country capacity. In analyzing the various challenges each organization reported facing in their response to Cyclone Nargis, we developed the four main categories, as well as several subcategories, to capture the similarities of challenges reported and quantify the number of times each type of challenge was reported. We then reviewed the lessons identified and selected those relevant to the overall categories and subcategories. Not all responding organizations faced the challenges reported or might find the lessons applicable.[2]

Restricted Access Delayed Response, Limited Coverage, and Complicated the Operating Environment

According to 13 reports, the time needed to gain access to affected populations delayed assistance and complicated logistics. The Government of Burma restricted foreigners from entering into and traveling within Burma. Furthermore, many responders had to negotiate with government authorities to operate in affected areas. Consequently, the response became highly dependent on nationals and those already in Burma. These responders and others who gained access were often overworked and operated beyond their mandate or outside their expertise.

Eight reports described transportation obstacles as further restricting access. Responders faced poor roads and infrastructure, high transportation costs, difficult climatic conditions, and remote affected areas.

Only one report cited the challenge of donor imposed restrictions, which prevented access to local authorities, limiting meaningful coordination and capacity-building. This challenge was, however, cited in several interviews with implementing partners. Some partners described restricted access to health workers, teachers, and technical experts as

---

[1]We reviewed 16 reports for lessons learned and 15 of those same reports for experienced challenges (see app. I for further detail).

[2]We did not attempt to assess the feasibility of the lessons we identified from the various reports.

particularly cumbersome. One UN Development Program (UNDP) official stated that U.S. restrictions significantly hindered the effectiveness of its development work in Burma. The inability to coordinate with Burmese government officials created difficulties for the USAID disaster assistance response team, one Office of Foreign Disaster Assistance (USAID/OFDA) official said.

The analyzed reports suggest that similar restricted situations call for creative approaches to negotiating with the Government of Burma and operational flexibility, such as the following:

- According to the Association of Southeast Asian Nations (ASEAN), the Tripartite Core Group was "an innovative example of a body that ASEAN and other regional associations around the world could replicate in response to future emergencies."

- According to the UN Children's Fund (UNICEF), although they generally experienced good working relationships with the Government of Burma, some negotiations were necessary. Discussions to gain access required skilled negotiation with support from Burmese nationals. UNICEF brought in their Burmese staff working in other country offices because they did not require entry visas and internal travel permits, whereas their foreign counterparts did.

- If a similar situation arises, the Protection of Children and Women Cluster recommends exploring alternative coordination methods to engage local actors that do not have Burmese government authorization to operate, without putting them at risk. For example, during the Cyclone Nargis response UNICEF was the only organization with a formal agreement with the Ministry of Education to carry out emergency education activities. The UN agency included other relevant actors in education activities through the cluster system.

- According to one NGO, the cluster system was initially effective in organizing responders, but geographical (rather than sectoral) clusters would have been more appropriate, given the restrictions on access and the inability of some organizations to reach affected populations.

- Boats and helicopters helped to overcome ground transportation obstacles and reach remote villages. However, boats were in scarce

supply and difficult to hire. For more effective future responses, one
report suggests that organizations could own or rent boats on a
monthly basis.

Complex and Poorly Managed Coordination Resulted in Disjointed Response Efforts

Coordination was somewhat difficult between headquarters (either in
Bangkok or Rangoon) and provisional field offices, according to 12
reports. Problems stemmed from limited telecommunication services, the
isolation of and weak leadership at field offices, unclear division of
responsibility between headquarters and the field, and poor
understanding of how information should be communicated from the field
back to headquarters.

Ten reports described poor information management and issues related
to data gathering as obstacles to coordinating, planning, or monitoring.
Difficulties stemmed from limited baseline data on affected populations at
the onset of the emergency, weak assessment structures and capacities,
and the restrictive political context. These problems were exacerbated by
some organizations' hesitancy to share information and a lack of
commonly used and readily available formats and databases for data
exchange. Many reports noted that shared information among responding
organizations was often inaccurate, unreliable, and inconsistent.
Communication among responders was also hindered by limited
telecommunications (radio, telephone, and Internet services) and
government restrictions on the importation and use of certain
communication equipment.[3] Internet access at field locations was
particularly problematic.

Six reports found that coordination among international humanitarian
organizations lacked coherence. These reports cited reasons such as
high turnover of cluster leadership, weak strategic planning and guidance,
and poor coordination of assessment and distribution activities.

The lessons we identified below emphasize the need for clearer guidance
on responsibility, increased support for field staff, and common reporting
formats:

---

[3]The Government of Burma controls and routes all Internet and satellite connections.
Also, the only wireless telephones that worked in the delta were Government of Burma
issued phones that had limited range and were not always given to international NGOs
and expatriates, according to one report.

- Coordination of future response activities could be improved with the use of statements of intent that clearly define each actor's role.

- The Emergency Shelter Cluster Review advocated for the replication of the "Bangkok-Yangon decision-making model" in similar emergency events, in which those outside the country provide logistical support and field offices have decision-making authority over operational matters.

- According to ASEAN, field offices were "indispensable" in providing strategic direction and facilitating coordination. To improve coordination between the field and headquarters, one report recommends establishing local resource centers and NGO liaison officers at field locations. Another report noted that increasing visitation and technical advising from Rangoon to the field would be helpful.

- Analyzed reports described the Myanmar Information Management Unit and cluster managed resources—including update documents, Google Group networks, and maps—as useful approaches to information management. However, the responsibilities of cluster information managers need to be expanded, including increasing coordination with the UN Office for the Coordination of Humanitarian Affairs reports officer and the UN Communications Group.

- Reports described the need for common reporting templates and information management tools to improve the consistency and reliability of shared information.

Some Decisions Based on Limited Information and Burma's Unique Constraints Hindered Implementation Effectiveness

Some shortsighted decisions by responders and Burma's highly restrictive operating environment hindered the effectiveness of some response activities. Ten reports cited examples of assistance supplies that were inferior in quality or incompatible with local conditions, which limited their usefulness. Examples included tents,[4] food, water treatment and filtration systems, information technology equipment, building materials, and fishing boats. Multiple reports and interviews identified U.S.-donated bottled water, tarpaulins, and medical supplies as particularly problematic. For example, DOD-procured water bottles were

---

[4]Tents proved to be inappropriate in Burma's hot and humid climate.

heavy and difficult to transport and medical supplies had instructions printed in non-Burmese languages. Generic packages, such as the Red Cross's shelter toolkit and the UN Food and Agriculture Organization's fishing gear, needed revision to meet the needs of local practices. Multiple reports credited local dissatisfaction of some aid commodities to poor participatory consultation and limited local procurement.

According to 10 reports, effective targeting and distribution of assistance was obstructed by political, logistical, or organizational capacity factors. Inadequate information about affected populations, logistical obstacles in reaching remote areas, and time and staff constraints complicated responders' efforts. The Burmese practice of redistribution within communities limited the efficacy of targeting: many Burmese communities would decide who received aid based on principles of fairness rather than need. Carrying out protection programs was also challenging in Burma, given the political sensitivity associated with individual rights. The Protection of Women and Children Cluster found it difficult to advocate for the inclusion of women and children in high-level strategy and planning.

Coordinating the transition between relief and early recovery activities was also problematic. Donors' focus on food and water distribution in the first months of the emergency delayed the initiation of and support for livelihood and economic recovery activities. According to UNDP, failing to target "medium to big farmers" exacerbated unemployment among the landless poor who depended on farmers for income. Interviews we conducted with NGOs confirmed weaknesses in livelihood responses, but also highlighted the same for shelter recovery.

Six reports found that procuring commodities in Burma was difficult due to factors such as inadequate supply and quality, lack of registered suppliers, and government-controlled supply chains. Implementing partners also told us the restricted banking system was a challenge, along with a declining exchange rate (with respect to the dollar), which made materials more expensive. Contrastingly, international procurement was costly and subject to Burmese government restrictions and approval. An interview revealed that USAID's food aid shipped from the United States took up to 3 to 5 months to reach Burma.

Monitoring, evaluation, and oversight mechanisms were limited in Burma. Three reports cite such contributing factors as the overall restrictive environment, remoteness of affected areas, inadequate staff capacity, and limited resources of local authorities. In one interview, an implementing partner explained that Burmese staff are reluctant to report bad news, which is an obstacle to reporting fraud or misuse.

The analyzed reports presented various strategies to improve the effectiveness of assistance through specific implementation efforts, such as the following:

- Reports described local procurement, incorporation of traditional practices and robust local engagement as strongly contributing to beneficiaries' satisfaction with assistance. UNICEF's water, sanitation, and hygiene division balanced this goal with the need to respond quickly by importing expensive goods only while local, low-cost solutions were being created. Reports cited rainwater harvesting, ceramic water filters, and earthenware water storage as successful local solutions. The Red Cross found that bamboo and timber shelter kits were better accepted than generic versions. With regard to fishing gear kits, FAO recommends supplying materials that can be used by beneficiaries to construct gear to meet their own requirements. Furthermore, nonlocal varieties of seed and livestock should only be distributed if local counterparts are not available. Because tents are inappropriate in Burma, UNICEF recommends developing and propositioning a "semi-permanent school kit" or temporary spaces that could be used as schools capable of withstanding the Burmese climate.

- Economic recovery should be identified and initiated as soon as possible after a disaster, with improved coordination of livelihood strategies between the Agriculture and Early Recovery Clusters. According to Save the Children, cash distribution and in-kind grants, such as those distributed through their Livelihood Quick Impact Project, were effective in promoting early recovery. In situations where markets were functioning, UNDP found that cash grants and cash-for-work were more effective than in-kind assistance.

- Targeting efforts should factor in the Burmese tradition of equity that underlines redistribution. FAO recommends engaging communities in discussions of aid and allowing them to decide how it should be distributed in a transparent way.

- The Protection of Children and Women Cluster Review describes the established Vulnerability Network as a creative response to the challenging operating environment in Burma prior to Cyclone Nargis but also states the need for a broader protection cluster to address remaining protection gaps.

- Analyzed reports also emphasized the need for improved
  procurement resources and processes, such as local market
  assessments, "preferred supplier" relationships for key commodities,
  and joint buying agreements. One report stated that a scheme like
  World Concern's Joint Procurement Initiative is potentially useful but
  only if initiated at the onset of the emergency.

- Technical field officer positions helped facilitate monitoring and
  interaction with implementing partners during the Cyclone Nargis
  response. One report recommends further building community-level
  capacity for monitoring. UNDP claims that at this level "diverse and
  representative membership," robust accountability systems, and a
  culture of transparency are essential to preventing mismanagement of
  assistance. In an interview, one USAID official stated that clear
  branding of donated goods was the key to effective monitoring in
  Burma.

Limited In-Country Capacity and Preparedness Exacerbated the Impact and Hindered Response Efforts

According to 13 reports, a limited number of experienced personnel and
technical specialists in-country had difficulty meeting all response needs.
The inexperience of some cluster coordinators created delays and
complications in the field. While local responders were generally better
accepted by local citizens and government authorities, they generally had
limited capacity and experience.

Seven reports describe local engagement in coordinated response
activities as limited, due to Burmese political, cultural, or capacity factors.
These factors included language and cultural barriers, lack of access to
electronically shared information, limited modes of transportation, and
inadequate time and staff to attend cluster meetings. Local responders
without formal operating agreements with the Government of Burma often
censored their input, which limited participation at cluster meetings.
International organizations noted time pressure, limited access to affected
populations, and lack of confidence in local capacity as obstacles to
engaging local actors.

The response to Cyclone Nargis was also hampered by weak early
warning systems and disaster preparedness plans at all levels—local,
national, and among international organizations. In addition, emergency
supply stocks and prepositioned food supplies were lacking within the
country.

Responders cited the improvement of in-country emergency preparedness and response capacity through personnel training and local engagement as critical. The following are recommendations culled from the reports that we analyzed.

- Many reports emphasize the need to build local capacity and better incorporate national actors into contingency planning and cluster activities. Standby arrangements with skilled personnel with humanitarian and remote management experience could be established by organizations operating in Burma. This should include a roster of local actors involved in the Cyclone Nargis emergency response who receive capacity training that is updated periodically over the long-term. One report recommends prioritizing local capacity-building in areas now under the responsibility of expatriates.

- Recommended strategies to improve local engagement included: training facilitated through learning resource centers in the field; appointing local counterparts for cluster leadership, such as information managers; providing Burmese translation at cluster meetings and for key documents; and developing alternatives to electronic information sharing. Engaging and gaining the buy-in of local authorities and other government actors (i.e., medical, education, and development affairs officers) is also key to facilitating local participation.

- A database of in-country information technology and communications support, suppliers, warehousing, and transportation providers would also be helpful.

- One implementing partner said that prepositioning relief supplies was essential, and noted the usefulness of doing so before Cyclone Giri hit Burma in 2010. The partner further suggested establishing reserve warehouses in Southeast Asia.

Appendix V: U.S. Agencies Experienced Challenges and Developed Lessons Learned in Responding to Cyclone Nargis

In responding to Cyclone Nargis, U.S. agencies experienced numerous challenges including Burmese restrictions on access to affected areas; U.S. legal restrictions; and difficulties coordinating, planning, and staffing activities. USAID issued recommendations to address the lessons learned from many of these challenges.

Burmese Government Travel Restrictions Constrained the U.S. Response

U.S. officials said Burmese government restrictions that limited their entry into Burma and access to Cyclone Nargis-affected areas constrained their response, limited their ability to assess needs, and made it difficult to monitor aid delivery. The Burmese government granted visas to disaster assistance response team members slowly and incrementally; with only 7 of 10 team members eventually granted visas.

Once in Burma, the team faced various travel restrictions and administrative barriers to providing relief, according to a team official. The official stated that he had to notify the Burmese government 4 days ahead of time to receive their approval for a flight carrying relief commodities to land.[1] He also had to provide a manifest of the commodities and persons on board four days in advance and to work with local partners to ensure they would be available to offload the supplies as the airplanes landed. Further, the Burmese government sometimes denied travel permits for USAID and other officials and set up numerous checkpoints in the early days of the response. The team also had to tap a wider breadth of resources to assess the extent of damage and need for supplies. USAID officials said that obtaining permission to travel to the Cyclone Nargis-affected areas remains difficult. They said that while the Burmese government typically grants access, the level of uncertainty surrounding when they will grant the access makes it difficult to monitor aid delivery on short-term notice, limits the number of site visits they make, and precludes them from properly planning monitoring visits. These officials said they would like to visit Burma and project sites whenever they want to monitor implementation.

---

[1]USAID/OFDA officials noted that this notification requirement is not unusual in many Asian countries; however the requirement is often waived in disaster situations. A waiver was not granted in the case of Burma.

U.S. Restrictions Limit Work with Burmese Government

USAID officials also said that U.S. restrictions limiting their ability to work with the Burmese government made it difficult to coordinate U.S. response and recovery activities. USAID/OFDA officials told us that typically the disaster assistance response team is able to work with the national government to coordinate a response. This was not the case in Burma and it created difficulties for the team. USAID officials told us that the restrictions on whom the United States can work with were a significant constraint and made it difficult to develop recovery programs. For example, in many villages midwives (who are government employees) are the only source of healthcare; therefore, not working with them makes it very difficult to improve health conditions in these villages. Some of USAID's implementing partners, including UNDP, said this constraint limited the effectiveness of their programs, especially in the areas of health and emergency preparedness, as they were not able to engage with key personnel. Some partners described restricted access to health workers, teachers, and technical experts as particularly limiting given the importance these officials have in their sectors. One NGO cited a reluctance to accept USAID funding given the constraints it would place on that organization's activities.

U.S. Agencies Struggled to Coordinate their Cyclone Nargis Response

USAID's after action report and our interviews with U.S. government officials revealed that U.S. agencies struggled to carry out a "whole of government" response. USAID said that while their response was based on humanitarian needs, State and DOD also had political motives which included engagement with the Burmese government.[2] Conflicting agendas resulted in coordination difficulties related to the appropriateness, timing, procurement, and distribution of aid. One USAID/OFDA official reported that once U.S. and international responders were allowed into Burma, competing priorities among U.S. agencies strained the response to Cyclone Nargis. USAID officials stated that in their opinion, DOD did not procure the commodities needed in Burma. For example, a company in Thailand produces mosquito nets that meet international standards. USAID asked DOD to buy nets from this provider. DOD originally agreed to do this but then later denied the request. They stated that the nets were not dense enough to fill the airplanes to capacity. Instead DOD provided items such as 5-gallon water

---

[2]In commenting on a draft of this report, DOD officials disagreed with USAID's assertion that DOD had political motives, stating their response was in support of overall U.S. humanitarian objectives.

bottles, which USAID stated are inappropriate for a number of reasons, including that people cannot transport them easily. The USAID officials stated that it was clear that DOD had different goals than USAID in providing assistance to Burma. A DOD official reported that all decisions on goods transported were made after consultations with DOD, State, and USAID officials. A State official reported having significant input on the decision to provide 5-gallon water bottles, as these goods had little risk of being misused.

USAID/OFDA officials told us that three USAID teams had to communicate effectively to conduct USAID's response—the response management team in Washington, D.C.; USAID/OFDA in Bangkok, Thailand; and disaster assistance response team in Burma—complicating communication efforts. USAID's after action report also cited numerous challenges related to information management. These included difficulty in communicating with the disaster assistance response team due to geography, limited available communication systems, and a lack of systematic reporting. The report also cited difficulty in tracking commodities because USAID/OFDA headquarters and the assistance response team used different tracking systems. USAID/OFDA headquarters used the standard USAID tracking tools, while the assistance response team had to use DOD tracking mechanisms.

As part of their after action report, USAID/OFDA issued numerous priority recommendations to address their communication and coordination challenges. For example, the report recommended developing a standardized commodity tracking system and setting up email accounts by position, not person to address challenges related to managing information. It also recommended developing an overall outreach strategy to raise USAID/OFDA's visibility and get information on USAID/OFDA's mandate, mission, and role as lead federal agency for foreign disaster response to key decision makers in other agencies, Congress, and partners in part to address the challenge of coordinating with DOD. USAID/OFDA reported that as of July 2011, it had implemented or was implementing each of these recommendations. For example, USAID/OFDA designed and implemented a formal in-kind grant agreement to facilitate better commodity tracking. In addition, USAID/OFDA is working on a video and resource kit for USAID/OFDA regional advisors and team leaders to use with senior U.S. officials in disaster-affected countries.

USAID's Planning of Assistance Delivery was Problematic	U.S. agencies reported challenges related to the planning and delivery of assistance as well. According to USAID's after action report, planning processes and products recently instituted for better response decision making were not well understood and did not meet needs. Some respondents noted a disconnect between planning and the flow of day-to-day work. Others noted difficulty understanding the purpose and timing of the Response Action Plan, a key planning document, stating that other tools were developed to track pending actions. Recommendations to address these challenges included a system for tracking day-to-day tasks in the planning process that may change more frequently than the response plan. Also it was recommended that USAID/OFDA's senior management team define the goal for the first response action plan in the disaster assistance response team activation meeting. Subsequent goals should be defined in the planning meetings and conference calls. As of July 2011, USAID reported that it had implemented these recommendations.
USAID Experienced Staffing Difficulties in Responding to Cyclone Nargis	U.S. agencies also experienced staffing difficulties in responding to Cyclone Nargis. USAID's after action report stated that staffing of response management teams and disaster assistance response teams were inconsistent and in some cases inadequate for the mission. Staffing seemed inequitable among the necessary field functions—over staffing some sectors, such as military liaison, and under staffing other important sectors, such as logistics. Also, USAID did not always follow staffing guidelines in response management policy and procedures, such as assigning staff with the necessary skills. Finally, due to the high demand for the limited number of specialists with specific needed skills, such as health and shelter, USAID/OFDA had difficulty finding technical specialists to meet all field needs. As a result, USAID/OFDA reported not having sufficient representation within all relevant sectors in the UN clusters, including the water, sanitation, and hygiene; shelter; and health clusters.

USAID developed the following recommendations to address the staffing challenges:

- The disaster assistance response team staffing process must be strategic, systematic, and deliberate. The team should drive field staffing requirements.

- USAID/OFDA should seek to expand the number of technical specialists available for field assignments at both the strategic and operational levels. Technical input within the UN cluster process must be early in order to influence the overall direction of the response.

- To the extent possible, USAID/OFDA should not put technical people in nontechnical roles, because it further reduces the number of available specialists when needed.

USAID reported that as of July 2011, it had implemented the first recommendation on the staffing process and was working on the other two recommendations. They stated that USAID/OFDA has worked aggressively to supplement staffing in key technical functions. This effort has included adding full time staff in areas such as health, nutrition, and shelter.

Appendix VI: Comments from the U.S. Agency for International Development

Note: GAO comments supplementing those in the report text appear at the end of this appendix.

The U.S. Agency for International Development letter was signed electronically by Sean C. Carroll, Chief Operating Officer.

Thomas Melito
Director, International Affairs and Trade
U.S. Government Accountability Office
Washington, DC 20548

Dear Mr. Melito:

I am pleased to provide the U.S. Agency for International Development's formal response to the GAO draft report entitled "BURMA: UN and U.S. Agencies Assisted Cyclone Victims in Difficult Environment, but Improved U.S. Monitoring Needed" (GAO-11-700).

The enclosed USAID comments are provided for incorporation with this letter as an appendix to the final report.

Thank you for the opportunity to respond to the GAO draft report and for the courtesies extended by your staff in the conduct of this audit review.

Sincerely,

Sean C. Carroll /s/
Chief Operating Officer
U.S. Agency for International Development

Enclosure: a/s

- 2 -

USAID COMMENTS ON GAO DRAFT REPORT No. GAO-11-700

General comments:

The report acknowledges the challenging environment in which the United States
Agency for International Development (USAID) programs have been implemented
and identifies areas where USAID oversight performance could be improved.
USAID notes that the report does not identify any significant deficiencies. We
also note statements that USAID took "some" actions to ensure that funds were
used as intended. Since these statements are followed by indications of monitoring
weaknesses, we feel that this does not accurately reflect the excellent efforts of the
team in implementing the programs in a difficult environment. USAID also sees
statements that "U.S. and UN agencies found little evidence that assistance had
been misused". We wish to clarify that the USAID staff has seen no evidence that
resources have been misused. We ask that Government Accountability Office
(GAO) consider the following changes to increase the accuracy of the report:

See comment 1.

- Summary, second paragraph and heading page 20: "USAID took some
  actions to help ensure U.S. funds were used as intended......but had some
  monitoring weaknesses". We request that the first word "some" be
  removed as we feel the USAID team performed extremely well given the
  difficult conditions, including lack of personnel resources;
- Summary, second paragraph; heading page 33, second paragraph page 33;
  and conclusions page 42: "U.S. and UN agencies said that they found little
  evidence that assistance had been misused." According to USAID, no
  misuse of resources has been encountered - we request that the word "little"
  be change to "no". Although there were a few potential examples cited in
  the report, they did not result in misuse. A closing statement on page 33
  indicating that there is no evidence that United States Government (USG)
  resources went to sanctioned entities would clarify your conclusion.
  Similarly, on page 42, we suggest that the word "some" is removed from the
  sentence "USAID has taken some actions to monitor its assistance and
  ensure funds have been used as intended and did not benefit sanctioned
  entities."

- 3 -

Recommendation 1: We recommend that the Administrator of USAID direct the appropriate mission and offices to improve management of grants related to Burma by taking actions, such as enhancing financial monitoring of agreements by including periodic reviews of grantee internal controls, transactions and disbursement records.

USAID concurs with Recommendation 1. It is critical that both project management and financial support staff take all necessary and allowable actions to ensure that implementing organizations have the necessary administrative and financial capability to implement USAID programs effectively and efficiently. While aspects of financial monitoring are addressed through pre-award surveys to determine organizational capabilities and annual financial audits, regular and continual oversight by trained mission project managers and financial support staff is vital. The environmental risk level, vulnerabilities, and potential weaknesses of the implementing organization, along with the nature of the assistance and the method of payment, are all important in establishing the level of appropriate monitoring given USAID's resources.

As noted by the GAO, USAID relies on independent annual audits conducted under the Single Audit Act, outlined in Office of Management and Budget (OMB) Circular A-133 for American non-governmental organizations (NGOs) and in the USAID Inspector General's *Guidelines for Financial Audits Contracted by Foreign Recipients* for non-U.S. NGOs. Significant financial review occurs at the headquarters level. Consistent with 22 CFR 226.53 subsections (b) and (e), NGO grantees are required to retain all award records, including financial, for a period of three years following the end of the award, and USAID has the right to unrestricted access of these records. In addition, the Agreement Officer's Technical Representative (AOTR) and field staff conduct award financial and programmatic monitoring through visits to observe program activities as measured against pre-agreed upon performance indicators, as well as through the review of quarterly financial and programmatic reports. The nature of an emergency response and the operational context (including access restrictions), however, can limit the amount of oversight possible. USAID reiterates its concurrence that financial monitoring is critical, and that financial reviews should be enhanced as allowable under OMB regulations. USAID will hold senior managers accountable to ensure that personnel perform financial monitoring to the strictest extent possible given the regulatory and operational limitations.

- 4 -

Recommendation 2: We recommend that the Administrator of USAID direct the appropriate mission and the offices to improve management of grants related to Burma by taking actions, such as providing grantees with specific guidance on the approval process for international travel requests, and ensuring that USAID staff monitor grantees' expenditures for compliance with related laws, regulations and grant agreements, including international travel.

USAID agrees with Recommendation 2. We request a clarifying statement be added to the report indicating that, with the exception of international travel, no evidence that expenditures not compliant with related laws, regulations and grant agreements has been encountered in USAID programs in Burma.

See comment 2.

Existing guidance on international travel, such as provided in the Mandatory Provisions that form part of each recipient agreement and are based on OMB Cost Principles, should be adhered to and enforced. The Agency's ability to conduct full pre-award surveys of organizations and timely audits should be strengthened. In addition, the role of the AOTR in monitoring programs and exercising their financial management responsibilities as codified in Automated Directive System (ADS) 303 and related documents should be enhanced. With that goal in mind, USAID has developed a number of training courses and certification requirements for AOTRs during the past few years.

Standard Provision on International Air Travel and Transportation included in USAID awards clearly outlines the requirements for the grantee to request approval for international travel. During the life of the award the burden is on the grantee to request international travel approval when needed, and failure to seek such approval results in noncompliance with the award's terms and conditions by the grantee, as well as the risk of cost disallowances by USAID. Although it is often difficult for USAID to remain fully aware of all actions by all grantees in challenging and dynamic post-disaster situations, USAID—consistent with OMB's USG-wide rules—relies on annual independent audits to detect instances of noncompliance and questionable costs. USAID will follow up as needed when questioned costs are identified by USAID staff or during the annual independent audits.

- 5 -

Recommendation 3: We recommend that the Administrator of USAID direct the appropriate mission and the offices to improve management of grants related to Burma by taking actions, such as reinforcing the requirement for staff to formally document site visits to grantees.

USAID concurs with Recommendation 3. ADS 303.3.17 requires and references the importance of site visit documentation by the grants' Agreement Officer (AO) or AOTR. USAID recognizes the importance of verifiable project oversight and concurs that documentation should be enhanced by all who perform site visits, including the AO and AOTR who are required to do so under the referenced ADS. In disaster response environments, the primacy of the focus on life-saving and life-sustaining activities can result in less focus on certain duties, such as site visit documentation, that are not directly related to the provision of immediate relief assistance. This does not, however, reduce the importance of documentation. USAID is developing internal policies to ensure documentation of all monitoring visits and their findings, with leadership in the field requiring overseas staff to submit visit reports documenting observations and concerns after each meeting with a grantee.

Recommendation 4: We recommend that the Administrator of USAID direct the appropriate mission and the offices to improve management of grants related to Burma by taking actions, such as ensuring all relevant offices are made aware of audit findings in a timely manner.

USAID concurs with Recommendation 4. The USAID's AO obtains audit information as part of the pre-award affirmative determination of the grantee's responsibility and may include special award conditions if the grantee is high-risk. Audit information is obtained from the Federal Audit Clearinghouse (FAC), a publicly available database, and other sources. USAID recognizes and concurs with the need to ensure that Contracting Officer's Technical Representatives (COTRs)/AOTRs are aware of any adverse audit information given their responsibility for monitoring. Audit information will be fully shared within the Agency in order to assist in assessing a new organization's capabilities, designing and negotiating proper controls, and verifying that internal control weaknesses are corrected to safeguard USAID funds during implementation and ensure that they are used for intended purposes.

- 6 -

Recommendation 5: We recommend that the Administrator of USAID direct the appropriate mission and the offices to follow up on the questionable costs associated with international travel that we identified in this report and take action as appropriate on any identified unallowable costs.

USAID concurs with this recommendation and will conduct appropriate follow-up actions with the grantee. In general, it is the responsibility of the grantee to obtain pre-approval for travel from the AO or AOTR. When a grantee uses grant funds for international travel that has not been pre-approved, USAID is under no obligation to pay for the travel. In the post-award A-133 or Recipient Contracted Audit, any cost for international travel that was not pre-approved will become a "questioned cost." Following the review and formal acceptance of the audit by USAID Office of the Inspector General (OIG), the Contract Audit Management Branch within USAID's Office of Acquisitions and Assistance will receive it in order to resolve all questioned costs with final determination by the AO.

The following are our comments on the U.S. Agency for International Development letter dated July 13, 2011.

GAO Comments

1. We acknowledge that USAID faced numerous constraints in conducting monitoring, and we recommend steps USAID can take to enhance oversight. We deleted the word "some" from before "actions." Regarding the statement in our draft report that "U.S. and UN agencies said that they found little evidence that assistance had been misused," USAID said no misuse of resources has been encountered. They requested that we change the word "little" to "no", which we have done consistent with the information we obtained. They suggested we report that "there is no evidence that United States Government (USG) resources went to sanctioned entities"; however, this conclusion is beyond the scope of our report.

2. USAID requested we clarify that, with the exception of international travel, we found no evidence of expenditures not compliant with related laws, regulations, and grant agreements in USAID programs in Burma. Our report discusses the questionable costs we identified from the selected transactions we reviewed. Our work should not be generalized to cover all USAID expenditures.

Appendix VII: Comments from the Department of Defense

OFFICE OF THE ASSISTANT SECRETARY OF DEFENSE
2500 DEFENSE PENTAGON
WASHINGTON, D.C. 20301-2500

SPECIAL OPERATIONS/
LOW-INTENSITY CONFLICT

7.5.2011

Thomas Melito
Director, International Affairs and Trade
U.S. Government Accountability Office
441 G Street, NW
Washington, DC 20548

Dear Mr. Melito:

This is the Department of Defense (DoD) response to the GAO Draft Report, GAO-11-700, "Burma: UN and U.S. Agencies Assisted Cyclone Victims in Difficult Environment, but Improved U.S. Monitoring Needed," dated July 2011 (GAO Code 320780).

DoD appreciates the opportunity to review your draft report and has no comment on the report's recommendations, which address the monitoring of grants in Burma by the U.S. Agency for International Development (USAID).

DoD wishes, however, to clarify for the record the USAID officials' comments on page 37 that were repeated on page 65 of the draft report. Specifically, USAID officials cited as a DoD goal in its cyclone response effort the political objective "to engage with the Burmese Government." DoD's actions were not motivated by an interest in engaging the Government of Burma, but were in support of the U.S. Government's overall humanitarian objective. DoD's provision of transportation supported the humanitarian assistance mission of USAID, which was the lead agency for the U.S. Government response to Cyclone Nargis, and the Department of State, which is the lead Department for Burma-related issues and policies for the U.S. Government. DoD's disaster assistance efforts were coordinated with USAID and the Department of State.

Thank you for the opportunity to respond to the GAO draft report and for the courtesy extended by your staff in conducting this review.

Sincerely,

Michael D. Lumpkin
Acting

Appendix VIII: GAO Contact and Staff Acknowledgments

GAO Contact	Thomas Melito, (202) 512-9601 or melitot@gao.gov
Staff Acknowledgments	Cheryl Goodman, Assistant Director; Michael Maslowski; Bonnie Derby; Ranya Elias; Elizabeth Guran; Kimberly McGatlin; Susan Ragland; Kai Carter; Ashley Alley; Sada Aksartova; David Dayton; Martin de Alteriis; Lauren Fassler; Will Horton; Etana Finkler; and Jena Sinkfield made key contributions to this report.

GAO's Mission	The Government Accountability Office, the audit, evaluation, and investigative arm of Congress, exists to support Congress in meeting its constitutional responsibilities and to help improve the performance and accountability of the federal government for the American people. GAO examines the use of public funds; evaluates federal programs and policies; and provides analyses, recommendations, and other assistance to help Congress make informed oversight, policy, and funding decisions. GAO's commitment to good government is reflected in its core values of accountability, integrity, and reliability.
Obtaining Copies of GAO Reports and Testimony	The fastest and easiest way to obtain copies of GAO documents at no cost is through GAO's Web site (www.gao.gov). Each weekday afternoon, GAO posts on its Web site newly released reports, testimony, and correspondence. To have GAO e-mail you a list of newly posted products, go to www.gao.gov and select "E-mail Updates."
Order by Phone	The price of each GAO publication reflects GAO's actual cost of production and distribution and depends on the number of pages in the publication and whether the publication is printed in color or black and white. Pricing and ordering information is posted on GAO's Web site, http://www.gao.gov/ordering.htm.
	Place orders by calling (202) 512-6000, toll free (866) 801-7077, or TDD (202) 512-2537.
	Orders may be paid for using American Express, Discover Card, MasterCard, Visa, check, or money order. Call for additional information.
To Report Fraud, Waste, and Abuse in Federal Programs	Contact:
	Web site: www.gao.gov/fraudnet/fraudnet.htm E-mail: fraudnet@gao.gov Automated answering system: (800) 424-5454 or (202) 512-7470
Congressional Relations	Ralph Dawn, Managing Director, dawnr@gao.gov, (202) 512-4400 U.S. Government Accountability Office, 441 G Street NW, Room 7125 Washington, DC 20548
Public Affairs	Chuck Young, Managing Director, youngc1@gao.gov, (202) 512-4800 U.S. Government Accountability Office, 441 G Street NW, Room 7149 Washington, DC 20548

www.ingramcontent.com/pod-product-compliance
Lightning Source LLC
Chambersburg PA
CBHW082145290526
45794CB00008B/3171